NIGERIA, IVORY COAST, SENEGAL – THE NEXT EMERGING COUNTRIES ?

Jean-Yves Naka

© 2017 Washington Publishing

All rights reserved. No part of this book may be reproduced or transmitted in any form or by any means without written permission from the publisher.

ISBN 978-1974614974

www.washingtonpublishing.net

Contents

Preface   P. 7
Introduction   P. 12

Part One : An economic, demographic and cultural overview of Nigeria, Ivory Coast and Senegal

    Economic and sociopolitical aspects   P. 16
    1 – Economic aspect   P. 16
    2 – Sociopolitical aspect   P. 23
    Demographic aspect   P. 27
    Cultural aspect   P. 33
    1 – General aspect   P. 33
    2 – Nollywood   P. 37

    Part two : The emergence of African countries

    Assets   P. 40
    1 – Cooperation   P. 40
    2 – Immigration   P. 44
    3 – Entrepreneurship   P. 49
        Private sector   P. 49
        Adama Bictogo, symbol of Ivory Coast's social capitalism   P. 53

Seduction for the « Made in Africa »   P. 58
Expansion of sources of financing   P. 60

Acquisition of new technologies in Africa   P. 65
1 – New technologies supporting
political governance and communities   P. 66
    Supporting political governance   P. 66
    Supporting the population   P. 71
2 – West Africa online interactions   P. 77

The next emerging countries   P. 84
1 – Nigeria and the MINT countries   P. 84
2 – Ivory Coast   P. 85
3 – Senegal   P. 86

Conclusion   P. 88
Endnotes   P. 90
Bibliography   P. 94

PREFACE

In discussing the future of Africa, some authors choose to describe the continent from an afro-pessimistic perspective, others adopt an afro-victimization perspective, while only a few embrace an afro-optimistic vision – we are currently witnessing a debate between advocates and critics of the African continent. For his part, the author of this essay endorses a positive view of the nascent development or economic expansion of some African countries, namely Nigeria, Ivory Coast (officially known as the Republic of Côte d'Ivoire), and Senegal, nations that according to him will be identified as «emerging countries» in the medium term. Jean-Yves Naka states that Africa is undoubtedly the continent of the future.

In this regard, the author focuses on analyzing the significant progress achieved by those countries, particularly in terms of their macroeconomic policies, economic growth and investment in technology (access to technological know-how). In addition, he highlights national development programs that support their commitment to meeting their development objectives by 2020.

The merit of this essay, which offers insightful intellectual thought inspired by post-colonialism, consists of presenting a paradigm centered on institutions, democratic governance, civil society participation, as well as the political will on the part of the governments of the three selected countries to attain the status of «emerging countries».

In this context, the author calls for the diversification of economic structures and African exports, which are currently over reliant on agricultural and mineral resources and subject to price fluctuations on international markets. Jean-Yves Naka advocates the concept of «made in Africa and for Africa» through the local transformation of basic commodities in order to create added-value products and reach self-sufficiency in terms of food at the local level. To achieve this, both private sector initiatives and traditional African commercial practices, which are essential prerequisites to becoming an emerging country, must be promoted. The objective is to put an end to the sad contrast between the huge natural resources reserves found in Africa and the poverty facing millions of Africans, which constitutes the «curse of raw materials».

African nations have developed more as consumer societies than production societies due to the preservation of the «rentier» economy (i.e. one dependent on raw materials) they inherited from European colonization, and their increasing reliance on imported goods.

According to Professor Sylvie Brunel, of the three most common notions about Africa – its extreme poverty, its exotic appeal, and its economic emergence, the young Ivorian researcher has chosen the latter one, thus expressing how determined Africans are to put an end to negative images of their continent and embrace a new optimistic vision for its future.

Using a neoliberal model, the economy in Africa has been growing by 6% annually over the past decade, a rate close to or equal to that of the Asian tiger countries, which provides a solid base for the future economic development of Africa. Indeed, the three countries selected for this analysis are potential candidates for becoming the new «African lions». These countries benefit from vast quantities of natural resources and are determined to develop their human resources, particularly through training and education, to which they dedicate one third of their national budgets, and without which sustainable development is impossible. In these countries, we are observing how natural, financial, and human resources are being mobilized on an unprecedented scale for their development, in contrast with many popular, overly general analyses that characterize many African countries as failed nations.

The author establishes a dialogue based on history, politics and the economy to set a context before getting at the heart of current realities, as political issues essentially stem from economic issues and vice-versa. This methodological approach is applied to Nigeria, Ivory Coast and Senegal, three selected West African nations which are candidates for becoming emerging countries.

The quality of this analysis, which avoids pre-existing clichés about Africa, puts the young Ivorian researcher in the category of post-colonial Afrocentric writers who believe in the present and future of this continent. His message incites us to reevaluate our perceptions of Africa based on new concepts. Furthermore, he presents an informed analysis of sub Saharan realities, especially those of West Africa. Jean-Yves Naka highlights the enormous potential of emerging markets in sub Saharan Africa and the development opportunities for both intra and inter-African trade.

One could fault the author for skimming over some of the situations he describes in the three countries, such as the dire consequences of neoliberalism in Africa, the African governments' elite «extraversion strategies» as defined by Jean-François Bayart, or the dependency paradigm. Instead, he focuses on internal dynamics (traditional loan clubs[1], Nollywood or the Nigerian movie industry, murid activities, infrastructure, automotive plant IVM or made in Nigeria cars, etc.), strategies that along with the «rentier» status of African economies, make them less likely candidates for becoming emerging nations. Moreover, he uses certain improper terms such as tribe, informal sector (qualified as «formalized anarchy»), etc., or flawed concepts such as the «Ivorian miracle», which proved to be an illusion, «lag behind in development» to refer to under development, and «illegal immigrants» to refer to undocumented immigrants. In a nutshell, those are terms used in academic literature either because of inadequate knowledge or for convenience, and also as a result of an unconscious superiority complex.

In addition, one could mention the lack of reference to regional integration, a *sine qua non* condition for the development of African countries, and the author's clear preference of the private sector over the public sector as the driver of development in a continent where both sectors (mixed economy) should cohabit well to address the numerous challenges it faces.

It is also necessary to note that this descriptive and concise analysis refers to a situation that should be taking place as opposed to what is actually happening, thus making it a politically correct essay. In fact, African progress, so glorified by its countries, is based on an economic growth principle that excludes any form of social development, meaning that growth is not linked to reduced inequalities or improvements in social justice. It only takes into account the price increases of raw materials due to a high demand by Asian emerging countries. Suffice it to point out that exports from Nigeria, a country that claims to be part of the MINT block (Mexico, Indonesia, Nigeria, Turkey) – as opposed to the BRICS block (Brazil, Russia, India, China, South Africa) – are composed of 95% oil, while the country is still importing 85% of refined oil for its domestic consumption. This represents a serious shortcoming for any nation that claims to be part of a group of emerging countries; therefore the debate is on.

Nevertheless, in praise of Jean-Yves Naka's work, which provides important information on the three countries, we need to highlight the author's recommendation that African nations need to continue to develop much stronger economic policies beyond the extraction and export of their natural resources in order to prosper, a fundamental aspect that makes it interesting to read.

Mbuyi Kabunda Badi

International Relations and African Studies Professor, and President of the Spanish Africanist Association

Introduction

Africa, a continent previously only marginally engaged in globalization, while continously greatly affected by various epidemics and atrocities, is gradually emerging as a more viable entity. All the countries that make up the continent appear to have a single common objective, that of attaining, as quickly as possible, the status of emerging country, using the model of the BRICS (Brazil, Russia, India, China, South Africa) countries. The traditional African model based on producing and exporting its raw materials has reached its limits and is being replaced by a world class structure that encourages the local processing of primary products into intermediate and finished goods. Creating added value within the economy has become the major goal.

We see more and more efforts deployed to support this profound change. The private sector represents the central point around which players operate to meet the growth objectives set by governments. The policy of simply asking western countries for hand-outs now coexists with the mobilization of internal resources to fund some investments. Entrepreneurship, which used to attract only a small portion of the population compared to employment in the public service sector, is gradually gaining ground. In its March 2014 annual ranking of the richest people in the world, *Forbes* magazine highlighted the remarkable ascension of Nigerian businessman Aliko Dangote, who in one year, went from 43rd to 23rd place on a global level. That same year, Nigeria achieved a gross domestic product (GDP) of some 568.5 billion USD. Also, the growth rate of Ivory Coast was among the highest in the world. In addition, according to the *Doing Business 2016* report issued by the World Bank, Senegal ranks among the top 10 countries in the world to have most improved their economy and this, for two consecutive years.

These facts, among many others, are indicators of the willingness and ability of Africa and its people to bring about change. They also signal that by leveraging the private sector, it can become more successful. Africa, with its large reserves of unexploited resources, undoubtedly appears to be the continent of the future. In this respect, the attention it is currently getting from developed countries speaks volumes.

This book provides an overview of the current situations that exist in Nigeria, Ivory Coast and Senegal, in terms of certain aspects of their economies, demographics and cultures. Some of the issues they are facing will also be examined, as well as options for becoming emerging countries.

PART ONE

AN ECONOMIC, DEMOGRAPHIC AND CULTURAL OVERVIEW OF NIGERIA, IVORY COAST AND SENEGAL

Economic and sociopolitical aspects

1 – Economic aspect

The 2008 financial crisis, which constituted a global «earthquake», has been one of the major events of the past decade. Did it, however, occur solely as a result of the combined collapse of real estate and subprime mortgages? The 2001 Nobel prize-winning economist Professor Joseph Stiglitz helps us to better understand the depth of this crisis in his book *Freefall : America, free markets, and the sinking of the world economy.* In it, he clearly demonstrates that the financial crisis was only one indicator of a deeper problem, that of the American economy. In fact, even before the stock markets collapsed, the American economy was experiencing a severe setback tied to its real economy. Contrary to the financial economy that only takes into account the volume of stock exchange trading, the real economy includes the volume of goods and services transactions. The author also draws an analogy between the causes of the American financial crash of the 1930s, also known as the Great Depression, and that of 2008. Their origin is quite similar; in both cases, it was about a shift in economic models. In the first instance, the U.S. went from an agricultural economy to an industrial economy, and in the second instance, it shifted from the industrial economy to the service economy. Some researchers, such as Richard Florida, also talk about a change to a creative economy[1]. These analyses help us to take a different look at African realities, in particular those of Nigeria, Ivory Coast and Senegal.

While Nigeria is economically different from the two French-speaking countries by belonging to the sterling zone as opposed to the franc zone for the two others, the structure and the operation of their economies share some similarities. In terms of their international division of labor, West African countries are known as the world's largest providers of raw materials, which are products with a only a slight added value. This situation, which is part of the colonial heritage of Africa, reached its limits in the 1980s. As far as economic wealth is concerned, Nigeria is the leading country in Africa. It is the primary producer of oil and its economy depends exclusively on crude oil exports; almost 75% of the national budget comes from oil revenues. However, before oil operations began to be profitable in 1968 from oil found in the 1950s, agriculture represented 55% of the GDP of Nigeria. Between October 1973 and January 1974, the price of oil rose from $ 3.80 to $ 14.70 per barrel, a 300% increase, which marked the beginning of the golden age for the country. In 1975, Nigeria was the world's main importer of Rolls Royce cars and champagne, together with Saudi Arabia (De Montclos, 1994). The oil market is generally marked by highs and lows, as the price per barrel goes up and down, either because of an expected shortage or oversupply of the raw material, such as when oil fields are discovered, for example. As revenues generated by oil increase, the economic dependence on oil increases as well. Based on this type of mechanism, a country's entire economy can be paralyzed if Brent and WTI indexes decrease. This is currently the case, as the global oil market is suffering with the discovery of U.S. shale oil[2] and its development since 2010. Between September 2014 and July 2016, profits from oil exports in Nigeria have dropped by at least two thirds. In an effort to mitigate the «curse of black gold», Nigerian authorities have opted for a diversification strategy.

A few kilometers away, the economic situation in Ivory Coast is very different. Since its independence and until now, the national economy relies on agriculture: coconut, cotton, rubber, and especially coffee and cocoa, which together represent the main source of economic development. Ivory Coast, with 40% of the world's production, is the largest producer of cocoa, and revenues from both cocoa and coffee account for 15% of the country's GDP. In 2014, the Ivory Coast's GDP was estimated at 34.25 billion USD, which is more or less 17 times smaller than the Nigerian GDP. In the early 1960s, the government fostered a national economy based on agriculture, since at that time the Ivorian President Félix Houphouët-Boigny was an avid farmer who wanted to develop his country's agricultural lands as much as possible. The cocoa trade is regulated by the International Cocoa Organization (ICCO) founded in 1973, following the United Nations international conference on cocoa. Its objective is to promote the fair and sustainable development of the cocoa industry at a global level for all participants.

In contrast to the Ivory Coast, the economy of Senegal is dominated by fishing and the production of peanuts. The Senegalese GDP was estimated at 15.66 billion USD in 2014, 36 times lower than that of the Nigerian GDP and almost two times lower that of the Ivory Coast. Surprisingly, the market structure of the fishing industry in Senegal is quite similar to the market structure of oil in Nigeria. Although backed by fishing agreements with the European Union since 1979, individual multinational companies are the main extractors of the country's fishery resources, whereas local firms only play a minor role in this regard. Due to a lack of funding, small local companies mostly use canoes to operate and cannot compete with multinationals, although they play a key role in terms of employment in Senegal[3]. The industry employs 20% of the economically active population. Thanks to European Union agreements, however, the fishing industry is dynamic and as a result, Senegal is able to obtain substantial tax revenues. Since the 1960s, the fishing industry has been considered as an activity that could supplement the agricultural sector should it be unable to produce expected results, given that the precipitation rate in Senegal is lower than that of several other African countries.

After the post-independence economic boom, called the «Ivorian miracle» within the country, an economic crisis developed, followed by a social crisis. This led to a recession in the West African nations, as the collapse of commodity prices impacted their financial resources. At that time, Ivory Coast was directly involved in the cocoa trade through a Price Stabilization Fund[4] and it categorically refused to sell its raw materials at market prices. This fund, however, was in fact buying commodities from farmers at a fixed price and then selling them abroad, regardless of the daily price fluctuations on international stock exchanges.

The Ivorian economic downturn did not only result from external factors as many authors contend. Leon Naka explained that some causes of the 1980s crisis were a result of internal factors, especially the careless attitude of borrowers towards the crippling credit terms imposed by lenders[5], which strongly impacted the agricultural sector. The primary sector was not alone to suffer from the consequences of the crisis. To help Ivory Coast and other African nations get out of debt, Bretton Woods institutions, namely the World Bank and the IMF, introduced Structural Adjustments Programs (SAPs).

While the purpose of these programs was to get African countries out of debt, they completely shut down the development of the secondary sector. Nigeria, Ivory Coast and Senegal had no option but to abandon the Lagos Plan of Action, whose objective was to establish a new African economic order based on food self-sufficiency and more regional cooperation. As commodities prices fell, however, the SAPs seemed to be the programs to adopt by African countries to avoid defaulting on their debt repayment. Such programs encouraged the adoption of more liberal economic policies that allowed more room for the private sector. Thus, national and foreign investors have taken the lead to achieve the governments' intent to process local products.

Although very different, the three West African countries discussed share a major common asset: their coast. Should domestic markets become saturated by local production, the export of processed goods, which generate added value, will be a new reality. For now, Nigeria still exports crude oil but imports a large quantity of gasoline. Ivory Coast produces cocoa but still imports much chocolate. Senegal exports large quantities of fish but keeps importing its derivatives. In Senegal, the tertiary sector is quite dynamic because of tourism. In addition to the exponential growth of mobile telecommunications in West Africa, tourism, especially beach/resort tourism in Senegal, plays a key role in the country's economic development. Tourism began to increase in the 1970s in response to the touristic boom in Africa's northern region (Morocco-Tunisia) and its eastern region (Kenya). Tourism is a unique activity as it fosters the development of other sectors due to an increase in overall consumption. In 2012, Senegal received about one million tourists, of which 42% came from France[6].

Another very «African» economic factor needs to be explored, i.e. the informal, or so called «non-structured sector». As defined by the Senegalese economist Mustapha Kassé, informal economic activities are « those activities that take place outside of criminal, social and tax legislations, and which are not included in the national accounting system ». The informal sector plays a critical role in the lives of a large number of Africans. The concept began to be popular in the 1970s with Keith Hart's 1973 work and since then, it has gained momentum. Today, it is very encouraging to see that more and more African governments are addressing this problem. As indicated in the French publication *Le Monde diplomatique* (2015), the French Development Agency revealed that in 2006, informal employment reached 90% of the Senegalese working population. The vast majority of households and small businesses do not use banking services for their daily transactions. In Ivory Coast and Senegal, for example, the banking penetration rate is only about 16%. In Nigeria, the rate is 36.3%, more than double that of the other two countries, but still fairly low. If those transactions were made through the banking system, it would make it easier to quantify their volume and grant credit to households and businesses.

Businesses operating in the informal sector follow a proper structure using their own standards, even though we tend to think that it is an anarchic society existing within the established society. The two French geographers, Alain Dubresson and Jean-Pierre Raison (2003) who focus on African human geography, have identified two categories of businesses within the informal sector – high-class and low-class businesses. High-class businesses encompass activities that require more capital investments, such as bakeries, transportation businesses, auto repair shops, etc. In those businesses, the owner is not the only one to benefit from the revenues of the business, but also its employees, since they help lower the unemployment rate. In contrast, low-class businesses are those that require less capital but also generate much lower profits. Their owners adopt survival strategies to conduct their operations. Looking at the overall picture, it is clear that public administrations and national statistics offices are not the only ones suffering from this *informalization,* because if employers do not pay taxes, employees won't get pensions later. However, measures taken by governments and banks, such as franchise taxes levied according to the size of a business, as well as the increase in mobile banking, seem to be effective ways to help formalize the structure of African businesses. Also, the sector is formalizing itself due to the expansion of financing sources. In the context of globalization, analysts are convinced that the informal sector represents an obstacle for obtaining foreign investments due to the under-evaluation of its potential. Currently, greater efforts are being made to modernize the economic system in Africa.

If we look more closely at the mobile or e-wallet banking sector in Africa, we notice that the development of this type of banking represents a gateway for people's economic activities. The difference between mobile banking and e-wallet is that the first one corresponds to the extension of banking services on mobile terminals. In West Africa, network telecommunications companies such as Orange or MTN dominate the e-wallet market, with the exception of Nigeria, where proper mobile banking services exist. The e-wallet, on the other hand, is a system that enables money to be kept in an account, linked to a mobile phone number, which facilitates financial transactions over a telecommunications network. The user of an e-wallet is not required to have a bank account or an Internet connection. The 2015 mobile phone penetration rate of 44.3 % in the region represents a positive sign for the development of e-wallet accounts on mobile phones. Ivory Coast is one of the biggest users of this technology, with a ratio of 6 million users out of a total population of 20 million in 2013[7]. The adoption of either the e-wallet or mobile banking may reflect the colonization types (French or British) that Ivory Coast and Senegal have experienced compared to Nigeria.

2 – Sociopolitical aspect

The deep influence that various European colonial regimes had on African nations in the past continues to affect the African sociopolitical scene to this day. The British Indirect Rule is based on a cohabitation system that gives the power to indigenous chiefs to run communities, while the more centralized French Direct Rule system is centered on a Governor. After World War II, nationalist movements in European countries leveraged the fragile post-war recovery to declare their independence in the 1960s. Most African countries, and particularly Nigeria, Ivory Coast and Senegal, became independent by means of negotiation. Surprisingly, unity among nationalist groups did not last long; as an example, the Nigerian political scene quickly experienced dissension. In Nigeria, there are three main ethnic groups: the Yoruba and Ibos in the south, and the Hausa in the north. These groups dominate the sociopolitical environment and, by extension, business in general. Religion is another source of conflict in the country. This ethnic and religious rivalry, which also exists in Ivory Coast but on a smaller scale than in Nigeria, extends beyond the political aspect, and other aspects will be examined later. In addition, West Africa has had its share of wars that, as always, are waged over two core issues: the question of «identity» and the unequal distribution of wealth. In 1967, the Biafran war in Nigeria resulted in the death of between 1 and 3 million Nigerians. This civil war was followed by a series of military coups whose objective, according to their administrations, was to restore peace in the country. In 1999, the election won by Olusegun Obasanjo marked the return of democracy. The Obasanjo administration made the fight against corruption one of its priorities and demonstrated its intent to end this situation by creating the Economic and Financial Crimes Commission (EFCC), although some critics see this powerful anti-corruption institution as a means to arrest political opposition members. From 2007 to 2010, Umaru Yar'Adua governed the country, until his death while he was still in office. Goodluck Jonathan, previously vice-president, then ruled the country for five years, in accordance with the order of succession.

In Ivory Coast, the years between 1999 and 2011 were marked by political instability, beginning with the first military coup of December 24, 1999. It was followed by a failed attempt to overthrow the president on September 19, 2002, which resulted in the establishment of a cohabitation system consisting of a united government representing all major political parties, which lasted until the 2010 presidential elections. Surprisingly, at the end of this election, two presidents were elected: Laurent Gbagbo, outgoing president, and candidate Alassane Ouattara. As no national consensus emerged, a post-election crisis erupted, which once again left the country in complete chaos, with an estimated death toll of 3,000 according to the United Nations. Since then, the situation has improved considerably and attention is turned to rebuilding the country, as indicated by the Ouattara administration's slogan: «The State Works for You». Like the EFCC in Nigeria, the «High Authority for Good Governance» is the new institution fighting corruption in Ivory Coast.

On the political front, Senegal remains the most stable country in Africa. From its independence until today, it has never experienced any military coup. After the country's independence, Leopold Sédar Senghor, the father of the negritude[8] concept, became the first president of Senegal. Then, from 1981 to 2000, Abdou Diouf ran the country, followed by Adboulaye Wade between 2000 and 2012. Since 2012, Macky Sall has governed the country according to democratic principles. Upon his election, President Sall established the National Office for Fighting Fraud and Corruption, the first Senegalese institution against corruption.

It is essential to know that the political style of governance in Africa has undergone waves of change. The one-party system in Ivory Coast ended in the 1990s, whereas in Senegal, it occurred in the 1970s. The timing difference could be interpreted as a difference in political preparedness in the two countries. One thing is clear, however: Africa has definitively curbed the use of military coups as a form of protest. The failed attempt to overthrow the government of Burkina Faso on September 17, 2015, which lasted only six days, demonstrates again that Africans are determined to achieve progress. This new African vision of stable state institutions and better governance continues to evolve. In this regard, the election of Buhari as head of the Federal Republic of

Nigeria on March 28, 2015 is truly symbolic, as the former president Goodluck Jonathan, a southern Christian, handed power to the elected president, a northern Muslim. Such a milestone has had a major impact not only in Nigeria, but in other African countries as well, because it occurred with no violence. In Ivory Coast, the election of October 25, 2015 follows a similar pattern of peace and political stability. The re-establishment of the African Development Bank (AfDB) headquarters, the implementation of the head office of the International Coffee Organization, and the massive influx of foreign investors to Ivory Coast are irrefutable signs of improvement in the business climate, further supported by the *Doing Business 2016* report for the region. In the current context of globalization, strengthening these components is important. And while there is a long list of challenges facing African governments, national agendas reflect their commitment to improving economic infrastructure, fighting corruption, implementing good governance and increasing access to education. Nevertheless, maintaining peace and security represent the top common priorities of the Economic Community of West African States (ECOWAS) because of the rise of terrorist groups and maritime piracy in the area. Beyond «politically correct» diplomatic agreements, we now see a more united continent that increasingly promotes a culture of results, despite its demographic diversity.

Demographic aspect

The various characteristics of West African populations, especially those related to their evolution, deserve special attention because they define the existing social environment. Once again, Nigeria is by far the most «different» country on the demographic front in the West Africa region. First, Nigeria is the most populated African country, with more than 177.5 million inhabitants, and ranks as the 7th most populated country in the world. However, the topic of demographics is quite sensitive for Nigerian authorities, as the «Revenue Allocation Formula», a component of the country's wealth distribution among states and local governments, is proportionally based on the size of their population. In order to obtain more funding, some local authorities inflate the population figures. As a result of this practice, all censuses since independence have created tension in Nigeria, which led the 1973 census to be invalidated and to protests around the 1991 census.

In Ivory Coast, the population is approximately 22.16 million, 8 times smaller than that of Nigeria. The population of Senegal, at 14.67 million, is 12 times smaller than Nigeria and 1.5 times smaller than Ivory Coast. Nevertheless, if we look at the ratio between the population size and the GDP of the three countries, in other words the Per Capita GDP, the difference is less significant. Population mobility, both inside and outside the countries, is due to population dynamics. The main factors affecting population mobility are linked to economic prosperity, improvements in living conditions, wars and health epidemics. On the one hand, there is economic prosperity that leads to greater buying power; on the other hand, wars and epidemics that cause populations to shrink. In Africa, while the consequences of malaria and HIV on the population are known, the recent Ebola epidemic indicated that better crisis management allows for better control over the spread of a virus.

In many developed countries, periods of high urbanization correspond to economic booms, such as during industrialization periods. Surprisingly, West Africa shows a different pattern in this regard. Despite the fact that we are talking about rentier states, in other words, countries whose main revenues come from exporting natural resources, we are currently observing an urbanization boom. According to the United Nations Human Settlements Program (UN–Habitat), the vast majority of the sub-Saharan African population will live in cities by 2040. The average annual population growth rate in West Africa is 2.7%. Although urban households tend to have fewer children than those in rural areas, their demographic growth index is higher. Using mathematical reasoning, if the difference between the mortality rate in rural areas and that of cities is higher than the difference in the population growth between villages and urban areas, this makes sense. In other words, if more people are dying in villages and fewer people are born compared to those in cities, the paradox holds true. To address this challenge, better living conditions are needed, which include better access to healthcare, sanitation, etc. Further, during crises such as wars, refugee camps are set up around agglomerations, which impact the urban growth rate, as the number of temporary refugees is taken into account to calculate growth estimates.

Lagos, Abidjan and Dakar are very dynamic urban centers. The city of Lagos alone has more people living in it than the entire population of Ivory Coast. The main reason for this situation is the influx of people from rural areas. For example, in Senegal, new generations of farmers who could have become successful peanut producers are packed in the slums of Pikine, because they all want to get involved in the tourist industry boom occurring in that city. Since population expansion and economic development are not growing at the same pace, many challenges are arising as a result of this imbalance. First of all, an unmanageable increase in urbanization leads to a rise in unemployment. Getting access to decent housing becomes increasingly difficult. While some people can afford to live in the elite area of Banana Island, where rental units can cost 9,000 euros per month, low income citizens in Lagos cannot find decent housing other than in slum areas. In most cases, slum dwellings do not meet the minimum construction standards, and there are no proper drinking water, electricity, or sewer systems. In Ivory Coast, there is a shortfall of some 400,000 housing units, 50% of which are needed in the city of Abidjan alone. In Nigeria, the high cost of living, security concerns, and endless traffic jams, called «go-slows», are urbanization problems caused by rapid demographic changes. Nonetheless, African governments are not ignoring this situation. They have decided to work hard to fix the problems, not only the obvious ones, but also the deep-rooted ones, with structural initiatives. Already in 2006 former Beninese Minister of Industry and SMEs, Professor John Igué, was qualifying the density of the Nigerian transportation system as «high and unique» for the West African region[9] as large Nigerian cities are well connected by direct flights and other means of transportation several times per day; something that is different from other countries in the region.

In recent years, in order to improve the mobility of both goods and people, Nigerian authorities have committed to implementing a very ambitious high-speed rail project spanning 3,218 kilometers at a total cost of 13 billion USD. The Nigerian high-speed train, which will replace the old train system, is positive for the country's brand image, as it appears in the top 100 world-class infrastructure projects identified by KPMG[10]. The first segment of the project, in operation since July 2016, covers a distance of 186.5 kilometers and connects the capital of Abuja with the city of Kaduna. This achievement heralds the beginning of the high-speed train era not only in Nigeria but in all of West Africa.

In 2015, Ivorian authorities invested 270 million euros for the construction of a new bridge in Abidjan, the third largest in the city, to relieve traffic congestion. The high cost of these infrastructure projects explains in part why the African development process is quite slow. In 2013, the same authorities launched a presidential public housing program to reduce the housing shortage in the country, which aims to build 150,000 low cost accommodations by 2020. Further, large cities are not alone in experiencing rising social issues. Development policies are expanding beyond the borders of agglomerations to the countryside, a sign of the government's desire to improve living conditions in rural areas. In developed societies, people living away from city centers in small towns still have a fair chance to work in an industry that interests them. In contrast, about the only choice for Africans in the same situation is to work in the primary sector because of their lack of literacy. This observation is not meant as a judgment on the quality of jobs found in the primary sector; it only indicates that the lack of literacy reduces the scope of employment opportunities. In addition, in remote areas, hygiene conditions are very inadequate and extreme poverty is common. According to the United Nations Childrens' Fund (UNICEF), an African girl from a family in a rural area faces twice the probability of being excluded from the education system compared to an African boy from a rich urban family. Paradoxically, most of the wealth of African countries comes from those areas where education is still a major challenge. In Ivory Coast, the Ouattara administration made school compulsory for children between the ages of 6 and 16 in 2015, a policy, among others, that aims to reduce the level of illiteracy among the population. Over the long term, education policies will greatly benefit productivity in rural areas. According to the French agronomist René Dumont (1962), the forefather of the French Green Party in France and well known for his fight for the development of African rural areas, since local peasants are more likely to endorse the development of their own lands and communities, they need to be better educated to become an opposing force to middle class civil servants and to defend their rights. They should focus their attention on adopting better agricultural policies, for instance. In addition to this «class struggle», more educated peasants would welcome the widespread use of agricultural equipment to enable them to save time and be more productive.

But how do you boost productivity without technology? To counter the lack of technology, rural households tend to have more children, as this represents a free labor force. Using this logic, the more children you have, the more productive you are, which also implies that you make more money. Obviously, this traditional mindset is not compatible with today's technological progress. According to Mbuyi Kabunda, the situation in

Africa generally results from the implementation of a faulty consumer model at the expense of an inclusive development model[11]. His so-called faulty consumer model means that society encourages people to make more money in order to afford imported goods which will help them become happier. Instead, the most appropriate African model should be to focus on the development of family-owned farms to enable them to become self-sufficient in terms of food. The current model, however, is geared on the development of industrial farming, whose main objective is to export raw materials to make money.

The harsh description of some of the current challenges in rural areas is not meant to show that Africa's development is stagnating or falling behind, but rather to present where it is now and how the drivers of change can allow them to be ambitious and nimble at resolving social issues. For example, African authorities are restructuring fragile foundations in non-urban regions, such as electricity. In Senegal, the government's 2016 national budget includes providing electricity to 400 villages to meet Senegal's Emerging Plan objectives, as follows: 136 villages powered by solar energy and 264 others powered by medium and low-voltage cables. Measures such as these that target remote communities help to alleviate the erosion of rural fabric caused by people leaving rural areas.

The management of demographic issues is a major challenge for African nations. Many stakeholders are involved at the local, state and/or federal levels, all working hard for a better continent, but they must be carefully coordinated so as not to step on each other's toes, and ensure that accountability and efficiency are maintained. Nevertheless, it is important to keep in mind that the African demographic picture is characterized by a young, culturally diverse population, which constitutes a great asset.

Cultural aspect

1 – General aspect

The notion of culture includes all the physical and ideological traits that characterize an ethnic group or a nation, i.e. a civilization, in contrast to a particular group or another nation. Since West Africa is not a country but rather a heterogeneous region, it has a wide spectrum of characteristics, such as ethnicities, languages, religions, and ideologies. Various population groups continuously interact, for example, Muslim Wolofs with Akans, who speak the Baoule language and continue to believe in witch doctors… It is on a «country» basis that we are evaluating the degree of similarity among various West African ethnic groups, because since the formal establishment of borders during colonization, the «country» has become the reference in terms of identity. Before they were split into countries, West African populations shared many common interests and values, which are still present to some extent today.

Common traits shared by the three countries include a strong spirit of solidarity and hierarchical structures. The African author Mamadou Ndoye (2006) has helped explain why African solidarity is so strong. According to him, group solidarity has developed to preserve and enhance family economic conditions. In the past, traditional African families acted more like economic entities. The more the entity grew, the wealthier it became. Thus, this scalable structure, which encompassed the family, the village, the tribe, and ethnic group, enabled the development of a real social security system. When members became old or ill, other more active members provided for them. Also, whether someone is from Nigeria, Ivory Coast or Senegal, respect is a key traditional value. This cultural aspect is very significant because with the economic emergence of the region, a number of multinational companies are coming to do business there, while having little knowledge of West African culture. A more local management style could be implemented if the senior management of these corporations wished to better integrate their foreign workers in the new environment. This is the reason why researchers such as my former professor Paul Sparrow at the EM Lyon call for the establishment of strong international management selection systems in order to maintain the effectiveness of values in the host country (Sparrow, Brewster, & Harris, 2004). According to Geert Hofstede's cultural dimensions theory, the distance index compared to where management is located measures the attitude held by individuals within an organization and their acceptance of the corporate hierarchy. Not surprisingly, Nigeria and Senegal respectively received scores of 80 and 70 on a scale of 0 to 100, which makes them highly hierarchical countries[12]. In the business world, non-acceptance of different management styles and hierarchy can cause employees to be passive, which can cause managers to exercise even greater power. African hierarchy is based mostly on age, although it also includes gender, ethnicity, skills, etc. Given this reality, should West African nations on the way to becoming emerging countries be encouraged to change their culture to better adapt to western business practices to become more successful? Looking at this statement from a different angle, changing people's beliefs and culture is in effect changing their identity. Doing so may not only prove to be extremely difficult but may also lead to all kinds of conflicts.

Respect for age is a traditional value based on the conviction that over time, elders have accumulated a wealth of knowledge and experience[13]. For example, in terms of family succession prior to independence, the eldest son was automatically granted both the right to run the farm and to make unilateral decisions for the entire family. Along with this power conferred by age, other relatives could not give their opinion on any matter. To show authority and intimidate, Africans use external signs of respect. For example, during their training in «centers» abroad[14], Africans learn to dress the same way as western executives in a suit and tie, and once they return to their own country they keep up the practice as a symbol of respectability. In the 1960s, Rene Dumont identified this as a newly acquired dignity, because Africans who had studied abroad wanted to show their superiority with this attire. Today, traditional African clothes are popular in the local business environment, especially in Nigeria and Senegal, and Ivory Coast is now also adopting them, in contrast to the country's strong French heritage.

The various phases that Africa has experienced so far have contributed to the evolution of the population's customs and driven the developing countries to adapt their rules and laws to better manage life within an evolving society. In this respect, in addition to the set of laws observed at the national level, in 1960, Nigeria, Ivory Coast and Senegal committed to conforming with international laws by adhering to the United Nations (UN) charter, namely Article 19 of the Universal Declaration of Human Rights that stipulates that everyone has the right to freedom of opinion and expression. Since then, protesting, criticizing or passing judgment publicly are no longer criminal offenses. However, preventing a citizen from enjoying this right represents an infringement to his or her freedom of opinion and expression. Ideally, the transition from the traditional model to the international model should have been automatic and its understanding, universal. Unfortunately, this new cultural environment is still quite fragile and has resulted in acts of violence and repression supported by political authorities towards groups of demonstrators. Protestors use many ways to make their voices heard: street demonstrations, written material, music, art, etc. For example, Fela Kuti has been an emblematic fighter for freedom of expression in Nigeria. He is also well known for creating his own musical style, the Afrobeat. During his life, he paid a high price for denouncing the political climate present in his country in the early 1970s, which included a dictatorship and corruption. In Ivory Coast, the singer Tiken Jah Fakoly is also well known for being outspoken. He wants to raise awareness about social equality through his reggae music. A strong pan-African activist, he not only criticizes abuses of power in his own country as he did during the last Ivorian political crisis, but also in other African countries. For example, during a rap festival in 2007 in Dakar, he asked President Wade (the Senegalese head of state at that time) to resign after his second term for the sake of his country. Senegal, for its part, stands out in terms of political stability, partly due to the role of major public advocates such as Youssou N'dour, who help maintain a peaceful climate. Former Senegalese Minister of Culture, Youssou N'dour has a huge impact on thousands of Senegalese, both through his music and his microfinancing bank, Birima, through which he promotes discipline in terms of money management. Known internationally, he also supports causes outside Senegal, such as helping to secure the freedom of Nelson Mandela in 1985. As poet William Congreve stated a long time ago, «Music hath charms to soothe a savage breast, to soften rocks, or bend a knotted oak». We can add that movies have a similar power. Pierre Barrot, an expert on the African film industry, said that Nigerian video productions, even if they were made under a military dictatorship, represent one of the most impressive freedoms of expression in Africa[15].

2 – Nollywood

When discussing the film industry in West Africa, Nollywood stands out as its biggest component. It is also one of the most important cultural vehicles of the African continent. Structural adjustment programs implemented by Bretton Woods institutions in 1986 caused various large scale projects, such as the development of the African entertainment industry, to be abandoned since it was more urgent to deal with debt. At the same time, surprisingly, the economic turmoil in Nigeria that was aggravated by armed robberies and attacks, and which caused families to hide in their homes, led to the boom of the home video industry. The term «home video industry» is often used to define the Nollywood phenomenon. Besides being produced within the limits of the informal economy, Nollywood movies and series are quite different from Hollywood movies: they have low production costs ($25,000 - $70,000), short shooting sessions (7 to 10 days for a video of 1.5 hours), their own distribution network, and a unique focus on the story at the expense of both the quality of the set and production.

The release in 1992 of *Living Bondage* is considered to be the debut of the Nigerian home video industry. Nollywood has evolved so fast that today, according to the IMF (2016), it represents a $7.2 billion industry as well as the second largest employer in the country, involving millions of people. There are more movies produced in Nollywood than Hollywood, a fact that indicates the dynamism of the ecosystem. However, even with more than 1,000 movies a year, Nollywood still lags behind Bollywood, the Indian movie industry, ranked as the largest in terms of productions. To increase awareness of Nollywood, in 2011, French researcher Claude Forest called for the Nigerian authorities to play an active role in the industry to help protect it from piracy and corruption, which are hindering the industry's development. Today, political authorities contribute to the evolution of Nollywood through regulatory institutions that aim to transform all participants involved in a production, such as actors, technicians and producers, into real filmmaking professionals over the long term, which means, in effect to move them from the informal sector to the formal sector. *Project ACT-Nollywood*[16] begun under Goodluck Jonathan's administration is an example of incentives granted to industry stakeholders, whose objective is to encourage the development of the movie industry in Nigeria.

PART TWO

THE EMERGENCE OF AFRICAN COUNTRIES

The concept of emerging economies refers to two situations, i.e. the economies of both under-developed and developed countries, as defined in accepted country rankings. In the first situation, these countries are striving to emerge and reach the level of those in the second situation, while in the second situation, the countries need to keep evolving their economies to compare with other countries within the same category. In this context, African nations have a long road ahead of them. However, the commitment expressed by African governments to achieve economic progress leads us to believe that the challenge of attaining the status of emerging economies is likely to be overcome shortly. Nigeria and Ivory Coast are aiming to achieve this status in 2020, while in Senegal the shift is expected to be visible starting in 2035. Additionally, political will is supported by a number of assets proper to each country.

Assets

1 – Cooperation

The preference of African countries for South-South cooperation at the expense of the traditional North-South model is at the heart of current debates. The bloc of South countries is characterized by countries whose development is lagging compared to western countries. Within this heterogeneous set, the BRICS bloc (Brazil, Russia, India, China and South Africa) serves as the reference for the rest of the bloc of South countries. Recently, economic development among South countries has led to some social and geopolitical changes. The G-20, broadening the G-8, allows for better representation of

South countries on the international scene and provides some assurance for better treatment when it comes to globalization. Unintentionally, current debates seek to limit globalization to the development of international trade. However, French economist Charles-Albert Michalet (2004) points out that it is important to add production mobility as well as capital flows to the exchange of goods and services. In fact, this «transfer of production» component constitutes one of the major factors in terms of the rapid growth of BRICS countries. The West Africa region, which includes a number of South countries, is changing very quickly; so quickly, in fact, that it is difficult to make predictions. In January 2013, we could still read in newspapers that economic forecasts such as that of Morgan Stanley were predicting that Nigeria would become the largest economy in Africa by 2025. However, only one year later, after some statistical adjustments, the Nigerian National Bureau of Statistics declared that Nigeria had already become the largest economy in Africa, ahead of South Africa.

According to the United Nations Development Program (UNDP), South-South Cooperation (SSC), also known as horizontal cooperation, is a process by which developing countries seek to meet their development objectives by sharing knowledge, skills, resources, and by combining programs or taking measures on a collective basis. SSC in Africa is often portrayed as an issue for black people, which is wrong, as it excludes the Arab populations of North Africa, who are also major players of pan Africanism. While SSC is quite popular today, it is not a recent phenomenon. In fact, it has undergone many transformations throughout its evolution based on the most urgent priorities present at different times. Professor Mbuyi Kabunda (2011) points out that this type of cooperation began in the 1950s and 1960s, in other words, during the Cold War. At first, it was marked by an ideology of national liberation against colonialism, as well as an ideology of non-alignment. Therefore, in order to strengthen unity at the political level, organizations were created at various levels, such as the Non-Aligned Movement, the group of 77 and many more. At the cartel level, Nigeria has been a member of the Organization of the Petroleum Exporting Countries (OPEC) since 1971. On the scale of the whole of Africa, many initiatives were also undertaken, such as the Lagos Plan of Action, the Abuja Treaty, to name just a couple. In 2012, the total value of China's trade in goods with Africa amounted to $200 billion USD, an increase of 13 times the trade value achieved in 2000, the year which marked the beginning of formal cooperation between the two. In a supply and demand scenario, players entering a new market try to differentiate themselves from existing competitors in order to satisfy the demand; in other words, they promote their competitive advantages. China is benefiting from the discord between the North and the South to find a way in. One of the numerous arguments with respect to North-South relations involves the non-reciprocity principle. If we look back at the 1990s, African countries dependent on the franc zone felt abandoned by the former colonial empire during the debt crisis. As a result, they were forced to devalue their currency, the CFA franc. Furthermore, during the same period, French authorities adopted strict measures to contain the migration flow from those regions of Africa to France. Paradoxically, Africans from the same regions were highly welcomed in France during the Second World War when the country needed soldiers. Nevertheless, it is important to remember that good relations between the north and the south are fundamental, as the development of SSC does not mean the end of North-South cooperation, but rather more options for African countries.

In West Africa, North-South cooperation, also known as vertical cooperation, takes shape through various forms of «regionalization» initiatives. The major ones are African Growth and the Opportunity Act (AGOA), a U.S. initiative, and the Africa, Caribbean and Pacific partnership with the European Union (UE-ACP). These partnership agreements foster significant trade increases between West Africa and the rest of the world.

Regional cooperation is flourishing and includes new dimensions such as intra-African trade among various participants: countries, companies, international institutions, non- governmental organizations (NGOs), research institutes, academic networks, etc. At the economic level, the idea of creating a common zone to facilitate trade within the region was necessary. For Samir Amin (2005), a well-known anti-globalization activist, it is quite impossible for «periphery countries[1]» to compete with monopolistic centers (the Triad) on a strictly national basis; regionalization must take place in a context that respects the sovereignty of periphery countries.

It is therefore on the basis of geographical regionalization that in 1975, the Economic Community of West African States (ECOWAS) was established, the main organization of West African South-South cooperation. It is a zone of free movement of people, means of transportation and goods, in which tariff and non-tariff barriers are removed. The total value of trade within the ECOWAS is currently estimated at $208.1 billion USD, with Nigeria alone representing 76 % of the total value. It must also be noted that a positive trend for regional trade has emerged, with an average annual growth rate of 18 %

between 2005 and 2014[2]. These economic indicators herald a promising future for West Africa, the topic of this essay. Nevertheless, extra-regional African trade is somewhat lagging due to various constraints that have not yet been sorted out. Akinwumi Adesina, the current president of the African Development Bank (AfDB), calls for African leaders to make additional efforts to improve trade conditions outside regional blocs. Although some advances in terms of the free movement of people are laudable, he encourages leaders to go further to better enable economic integration by removing tariff and non-tariff barriers to trade among different regional blocs in Africa[3]. This way of thinking essentially favors immigration.

2 – Immigration

The migration phenomenon is considered an important component of a country's economic growth. For Mbuyi Kabunda, immigration should also be seen as an opportunity for the host country[4]. Beyond the image of human solidarity attributed to the host country, both parties benefit from each other because of increased diversity and differences in ways of thinking. The case of West Africa constitutes proof of what the eminent Congolese professor stated earlier. In West Africa, although immigration to industrialized countries generates most of the attention, it is regional migration that has always primarily characterized the movement of people. Starting in the 15th century, the Mandings coming from northern territories (now known as Mali) began to settle in the north of Ivory Coast, particularly around the cities of Kong and, later, Odienne. Then, around 1690, on the east coast of Ivory Coast, the Abrons left their lands (now known as Ghana) and settled in the Zanzan region, mainly in the city of Bonduku, before establishing their own kingdom, the Gyaman Kingdom. During the colonial era, French colonists based in Ivory Coast, then considered a pillar of French West Africa[5], obtained a significant proportion of their workforce from Burkina Faso (then known as the Republic of Upper Volta) to fill the shortage of workers needed to develop small existing industries. Later on, many more foreign workers were needed as the country began intensive work to build their road and rail networks. In 1951, a formal organization was established, the SIAMO[6], to better manage the flow of workers and it has documented that at least 230,000 Burkinabes contributed to the construction of Ivory Coast's infrastructure. The migration movement continued to expand after independence as a result of the welcoming immigration policy of President Felix Houphouet-Boigny. This open policy was in line with the vision of the Ivorian president, which he called a Revolution without the « R[7] ».

Through these historical facts, one can see that immigration has contributed significantly to the development of Ivory Coast. According to the 2014 population census, foreigners represent 24.2 % of the country's inhabitants. We therefore believe that with an orientation of this magnitude towards immigration, Ivory Coast is on the right track to become an emerging country in the near future. Using the push and pull theory, we can highlight a few factors that influence intra-regional migration flows. Those are factors that on one hand push people to leave a certain place, and on the other, factors that attract populations to move to a better environment. In the first instance, political instability, unemployment, wars and social division give people reasons to leave their home. In the second instance, besides cyclical factors, some structural factors are taken into account such as higher salaries in other locations.

In 1967, the Biafra war broke out in Nigeria, which lasted three years. Also known as the Nigerian civil war, this war resulted in numerous deaths and represented a migration factor for many Nigerians. For the sake of unity, General Yakubu Gowon, then head of the federal military government, fought Odumegwu Ojukwu, the leader of the secessionist state of Biafra on all fronts: military, political and economic. On the economic front, sanctions such as the naval blockade and the currency change in January 1968 contributed to strangling the Biafran region. For example, the price of meat increased twenty-fold, going from 3 shillings to 60 shillings per pound, while the price of dried fish increased twelve-fold, going from 5 to 60 shillings per pound. This sharp jump in the inflation rate made life difficult for numerous Nigerians. It is estimated that more than 3 million of them fled the country for neighboring provinces and countries such as Cameroon. Odumegwu Ojukwu himself found asylum in Ivory Coast for quite a long time. Generally, the vast majority of Africans, particularly those seeking to leave their home countries, immigrate to other African countries, even though public opinion may lead us to believe that they are immigrating to Europe. During the Valletta summit on migration in November 2015, Senegalese President Macky Sall pointed out that countries in the West respond fiercely to African immigration although in fact, it represents a minor issue. Unfortunately, such an attitude from EU governments contribute to reinforcing the myth of significant African immigration to Europe. According to the World Bank, more than 38% of migrants worldwide left a developing country for a similar country in 2013, whereas 34% moved from a developing country to an industrialized country. Further, the movement of people within countries of the South may well be underestimated by the UN due to a lack of reliable sources, and the gap between the two trends may be much more significant[8]. Illegal immigration is the one aspect that represents an infringement of the law and misrepresents the movement of Africans around the globe; as a result, people tend to put all immigrants in the same basket. It is true that some Africans choose the illegal immigration track under the pretense of having scarce opportunities for employment and self-development in Africa. While the reasons given may be legitimate, they still cannot justify those risky ventures, as too many regions are experiencing the same limited opportunities. Regardless of how much effort African governments are making to improve their economic situations, there will always be population groups that will remain dissatisfied. The case of Saada Ndiaye, a 32-year-old Senegalese man, illustrates this point. For 500 euros, this talented young carpenter and tradesman chose to risk his life to make his way illegally to the Spanish coast, under the illusion that Europe is a piece of heaven[9]. What we have discovered is that candidates for illegal immigration are neither looking for jobs nor do they have the intention of making a better life for themselves in Africa. Instead, they seek to immigrate to Europe by all means possible because on one hand they are pressured by their families, and on the other hand, they are afraid of being mocked or labelled as cowards by their entourage, since few succeed at crossing the Mediterranean. African countries are strongly opposed to those practices because for them, the consequences are serious. In addition to seeing its image tarnished, Africa is seeing a decrease of its working population and an increase in the debt of families needing to finance the illegal journeys of their relatives. This situation is a bit ironic, because skills demonstrated by illegal immigrants i.e. courage and determination, are qualities that African Human Resources managers are looking for! As mentioned earlier, regional immigration is much more significant than international immigration and as a result of the ECOWAS 1979 legal framework[10], people within the region have no travel restrictions. High economic growth of countries in a region can lead to the creation of some activity hubs and as a result, attract numerous foreign nationals to those hubs (as is the case in South Africa). According to the International Organization for Migration (2013), those countries in West Africa are Nigeria, Ivory Coast, Senegal and Ghana because their political, sociocultural and economic perspectives are interesting enough in the eyes of migrants in terms of prosperity and integration in the new environment. Major cities such as Lagos, Abuja, Abidjan, Dakar and Accra are getting ready to host new residents. This illustrates once again how important immigration is in building strong nations. West Africa needs all of its people to help convert those economic figures into development achievements. Ivorian businessman Stanislas Zézé invites not only Africans living in the continent, but also the African diaspora, to return to help build their countries without waiting for any sort of «guarantee» as they always respond, because before they left this was not part of the deal[11]. This is in some ways a call for entrepreneurship.

3 – Entrepreneurship

Private sector

« It is an obvious truth to say that investment is the major driver of growth and development» (Naka, 1989). Since the advent of neoliberalism, business plays a central role in the development of a country. Entrepreneurship as a way of reducing poverty is no longer wishful thinking but a reality. In West Africa, the culture of entrepreneurship is spreading everywhere, in the same manner as the economic climate is getting healthier. «Africa is on the move» said former U.S. President Barack Obama at the sixth annual Global Entrepreneurship Summit held in 2015 in Kenya. Cameroonian professor Lucas Pony (2011) considers that opening a business is a great venture for those motivated to demonstrate the required skills: determination, a willingness to break down barriers, persistence, emotional resilience, good health, common sense, wisdom, curiosity, open-mindedness, empathy, enthusiasm, etc. Noteworthy is that in West Africa, the business culture is more developed in English-speaking countries than in French-speaking ones. We believe that this situation has been influenced by the differences between the direct rule and the indirect rule models used during colonization. Nigeria produces more business people than all the countries of West Africa combined, and that has been the case for ages. Some experts like Marc-Antoine Perouse de Montclos describe Nigeria as the haven of wild capitalism and freedom of free enterprise (1994). Colonization belongs to the past, so Africans have no power to change it. However, they still have the power to write new pages of their history and prepare for a better future by adopting entrepreneurial behaviors. The reason why we are so optimistic that Nigeria, Ivory Coast, and Senegal will become the next emerging countries is that today, the new African generation is becoming empowered by the «African Dream», a concept that encourages people to channel their creativity into concrete achievements to take charge of their continent. It is difficult to imagine that in Nigeria, the sixth biggest oil exporter in the world, there are gasoline distribution problems within its own borders. It is true that we do not necessarily make the connection between the production of crude oil, which must then be refined to make gasoline. The frequent shortages of gasoline at service stations cause social upheaval among Nigerian consumers and also make way for the development of a black market, within the informal economy. We could assume that the transportation sector is the only one affected by this situation, but since a large number of Nigerian families and businesses rely on diesel for their power generators, the magnitude of this crisis is huge —no cars and no power. In this country where the price of fuel is subsidized, when authorities and oil companies do not agree on the subsidies, social unrest erupts, as prices become volatile and gas stations empty. The reasons why fuel subsidies were implemented in 1973 are admirable, as the objective is to have a uniform price regardless of which region one lives in. This is a common practice in oil-producing countries and Nigeria did not want to be the exception.

This scenario was similar to the role played by the Price Stabilization Fund in Ivory Coast for developing the farming sector. Unfortunately, the subsidies that were supposed to support low-income people failed to achieve that objective due to a high level of corruption. Therefore, in 2016, the Buhari administration decided to abolish fuel subsidies and allocate those funds to other priorities. Between 2006 and 2015, the government spent almost $40 billion USD in fuel subsidies[12]. Instead of allocating such an enormous amount of money to stabilize the price of gasoline, more investments could have been made in other sectors such as health and agriculture. In 2015, for example, the budget for fuel subsidies was more than double the budget for education[13]. We believe that this government decision will help liberalize the oil industry, leaving the market to determine prices. One of the main objectives of this book is to demonstrate that as the private sector becomes more and more active in our region, Africa will become self-sufficient. In this period of change, Nigerian billionaire Aliko Dangote stands out – he wants his country to stop relying on imports. After his success story in the cement industry, Dangote is getting involved in the oil business to address the frequent shortages of fuel in the country. Today, Nigeria imports about 85% of its domestic oil consumption. Dangote will be the first entrepreneur to establish a large scale local refinery. His refinery will have a capacity of 650,000 barrels/day, the fifth largest refinery in the world after those in Venezuela, South Korea and India. Current refineries in Nigeria can produce 445,000 barrels/day, but because of a lack of maintenance, they are underutilized. Dangote's plant will be operational in 2018, and starting in 2019, it will be able to produce 55.2 million liters of fuel daily[14]. Together with Nigerian professor Patrick Utomi, we believe that Dangote's refinery will empower others to further develop the oil industry and also reduce people's anxieties about such a basic commodity[15].

In addition to the actions of national business champions, the increase of regional trade within the ECOWAS is supported by forces outside the area. As Dr.

Folashade Soule-Kohndou (2013), clearly states, South-South relations are no longer merely centered on an ideology, or limited to the political and government spheres. The concept is becoming more popular and now involves the private sector. For example, with the rise of pan-African bank activities, banks share their local and regional knowledge to offer products and services more adapted to their growing customer base. In November 2015, we had the privilege of meeting Moroccan investment banker Youssef Benkirane in Casablanca, who reinforced our view as to the growing role that companies such as banks play in the development of South-South cooperation. BMCE group, the Moroccan financial entity he works for, acquired 35% of the West-African group Bank of Africa in 2007 and gradually increased its stake until in 2015, it owned 75% of the shares. According to Mr. Benkirane, Africa has many assets that vary from one country to another in terms of their bureaucratic, economic and social aspects. Therefore, rather than using a one-size-fits-all approach, companies are adapting their offers based on local situations, using both the latest available technologies and success stories in similar regions. In his sector, mobile banking is a leading high-tech tool that enables banks to reach a public thus far excluded from the banking system. The BMCE group is already present in 18 African countries and aims to expand its presence to the 55 countries of the continent by 2025. This vision reflects the pan-African mindset adopted by the following African businessman.

Adama Bictogo, symbol of Ivory Coast's social capitalism

In our view, the success story of businessman Adama Bictogo highlights the key role played by the private sector in developing West Africa. Bictogo is the CEO of Snedai Group, a conglomerate which embodies the current transformation program of Ivory Coast. He is considered a symbol of social capitalism in the country, as he has committed to propel his company forward in a way that addresses social inequalities in Ivory Coast. His group operates in four areas – technology, transportation, energy and construction. A few days before I met with him, he signed an agreement with the government for building a 700-megawatt clean coal plant for about $1.34 billion USD. As you know, businesses are regulated by a number of factors. In Bictogo's case, his discipline is undoubtedly a factor in terms of his company's leadership. He usually starts his day at 4 A.M. and finishes at 8 A.M. Such a short day, right? In fact, this four- hour period, during which he goes jogging before meditating and then making the day's decisions represents his most precious time of the day as he is in deep immersion. The rest of his day represents a consolidation of the 4-hour period. As a child, he had extraordinary numerical skills and his family saw him as a future engineer. Instead, he wanted to be either a bank director, a company general manager or an Army general. His destiny changed, however, when his parents sent him to finish high school in France. Once there, young Adama began to socialize with Jewish students and he discovered his passion for entrepreneurship while spending time in his friend's family businesses. Entrepreneurship was a vocation «sleeping» in him. He knew he would appear disgraceful to his family, a notable family of farmers in the south of

Ivory Coast, if he decided to drop out of school and get into the business world after high school. At that time, and to some extent today, notable families sent their children abroad to get a good education, but it was in fact a form of «keeping up with the Joneses». In order for the family to show off, the children needed to get back home with the best grades and a world-class degree. This is what Adama ended up doing. He came back to Ivory Coast in his mid-twenties with a Master's degree in Strategy and Business Administration. He worked three years in mass-market retail in a company named Score, where he implemented the discount model. At that time, in 1992, the consumer population was quite polarized between high and low income classes. The first category was shopping in supermarkets, while the second category was shopping in local markets. Although he could not create a middle class, Adama was convinced that by developing such a sales model in Ivory Coast, he could transform the low income class into supermarket shoppers. It may seem obvious today but at that time the country was so divided that it was unthinkable. With the success of his initiative, he quit his executive position to open his first business importing fresh goods. His business did well until 1999, when the country experienced its first military coup. At that time, Snedai's idea was not born yet. During this period of instability, Bictogo made an analysis of the weaknesses of African firms. According to him, companies go bankrupt 30% of the time because they lack cash flow, while 70% of the time because they lack human resources capacity. Managers tend to overlook employee satisfaction and their ability to face challenges to focus on numbers, sales and growth instead.

    Another success factor is Snedai's reliance on the collective effort, i.e., the team effort. Apart from being known as one of the most innovative companies of the 21st century, Google is one the greatest workplaces in the world because of its working environment and the amazing benefits it provides to employees: abundant perks, free fitness classes, gym memberships, on-site massages, etc. As a result, the company attracts the top talents. In Ivory Coast, Snedai is doing the same thing. While there is no ranking of great places to work in the country, Snedai would no doubt hold first place. It pays its people twice the average salary in the industry. The reason why it spends a «premium price» on employees is because management wants them to be able to afford good professional attire and reliable means of transportation. On the other hand, they are less tolerant of employees who do not respect the dress code or arrive late. I remember the day I was with Bictogo in his lavish glass and wood office – he had just hired three graduate engineering students from the Felix Houphouet-Boigny national polytechnic institute, a top university in Ivory Coast. Snedai's vision of building a «center of excellence» makes his a leading company in the country.

National development plans in Nigeria, Ivory Coast and Senegal aim to turn these countries into emerging nations with the support of local companies through public/ private partnerships. These programs have been carefully developed, unlike the «Zaireanisation» efforts under Zaire's former president Mobutu Sese Seko. In 1973, in the current Democratic Republic of Congo, Mobutu signed a measure allowing the state to seize all foreign-owned farms and companies to give them to Zairians. It was a somewhat foolish move to empower the Congolese elite to manage their own business environment in the interest of the nation. Thousands of businesses valued at around $1 billion USD at the time were distributed among top officials and their friends and relatives. It was a complete man-made disaster. Many new owners, perhaps too busy buying the latest imported Mercedes-Benz, discovered that they had neither the skills, the time nor the interest to run their companies. Within one year, this naive nationalism-based projection plunged Zaire into an unprecedented economic crisis, a situation worsened by the decline of copper prices, the country's main source of revenue. Michela Wrong, a British news correspondent in Zaire at the time, witnessed businesses closing, prices rising, people being laid off, and shelves in stores being emptied. What we are seeing in West Africa at the moment has nothing in common with this madness. Today, African governments are empowering local entrepreneurs through some layers of protectionism to encourage them to invest more. In this regard, Bictogo has advised various head of states in the region to keep doing so, including President Ouattara of Ivory Coast, for the reason that it is a prerequisite to meeting the objectives of the Ivory Coast National Development Plan (2016-2020). As well as being a successful businessman, Adama is also a political leader, and his close relationship with President Ouattara has subjected him to a lot of criticism. Rumors have been spreading that he unfairly gets favors from the president. However, when he first met President Ouattara on February 14, 1994, he could not imagine that this man would be head of state one day. In life, connections help, but is friendship alone enough to make someone successful? We do not believe it! If it were true, the Mobutu Zaireanisation would have created successful and sustainable pan-African companies. Instead, we consider connections as external factors and in the case of Bictogo, a non-negligible one. African governments give additional incentives to businesses having either the ability to make countries self-sufficient in one field or to those with a particular expertise that can be linked to the country's reputation. For example, the city of Abidjan has a population of about 5 million, but with an urbanization rate of 50%, transportation is becoming a problem. Nearly 88% of the population relies on public transportation. People are constantly stuck in traffic as they use roads to move from place to place. While waiting to implement a metro system in 2019, the authorities decided to develop water buses such as those used in Dubai or Venice. Abidjan has a unique asset as it is crossed by the Ebrie lagoon, which borders various districts of the capital and covers a distance of 150 km. Since 1980, the state-owned company Sotra has introduced water buses, but due to a lack of funding, the operation has not evolved as fast as demand. Today, there is demand for about 300,000 passengers/day, of which Sotra can only meet 10%. In 2015, the government cancelled Sotra's exclusive right to operate on the lagoon to enable two 100% Ivorian competitors to enter the market. Among the newcomers is Société de Transport Lagunaire (STL), part of the Snedai group, that has been granted a 25-year operating license. STL began operations in 2017 with a fleet of 16 boats and will gradually increase that to 45 boats over the next four years. STL gives its customers the option of buying tickets online, an innovation in Ivory Coast transportation. Once fully operational, the water bus company alone would be able to meet a least 17% of the demand and generate 400 direct new jobs.

STL is one of many projects to foster a «pure Made in Africa» movement.

Seduction for the « Made in Africa »

According to Malian author Musa Konate, real human development is the development of the people, by the people and for the people[16].

At the core of business development in Africa is the expansion of the middle class or, in better terms, the consumer class. The lack of consensus about its definition reflects the challenge to assess its real size. However, if we approach this concept on a revenue basis, the African Development Bank (2012) estimates that the middle class in Africa encompasses people whose revenues vary between $2 and $20 per day per person, for a total of approximately 300 million of people across the continent. Since this definition was developed based on African realities, African business men and women bear the responsibility to make things happen. For this reason, Kabunda (2011), warns African companies against seeking excessive profits because it can lead them to compete on international markets where they have few competitive advantages. Today, more and more Africans are becoming involved in strengthening the intracontinental trade. Most visible are those who operate in the retail sector, including food, fashion, transportation, etc. Other less visible participants put their fears aside to venture into niche markets. As a result of this growing entrepreneurial spirit, the automotive industry is emerging in the region. The Nigerian Innoson Vehicle Manufacturing Company (IVM) meets a growing local demand with its trucks, buses and SUVs. Improving the quality of the transportation environment with the first *Made in Nigeria* cars represents a considerable challenge for Innocent Chukwuma, CEO of Innoson Group; new *Made for Africa* cars are far better adapted to local roads and cost the same as buying used imported cars. With a budget of $7, 000 USD, people can afford a new IVM car. So far, most of the parts are sourced locally except for the engine and the backbone chassis, which are still imported. The automobile industry experienced a great boom during the industrial period of the 20th century in industrialized countries, a period marked by mass production. In Spain, historian Jordi Maluquer De Montes (2014) characterizes this period in his country as the «revolución de 600», which refers to the huge social impact made by the 600 model of car manufacturer Seat. The economic and social impact of IVM cars will gradually reach the West Africa region, the entire continent and then, who knows, the world...

Rating agencies play a key role in the development of countries because they assess the solvency of organizations and other economic players. If they fail in their mission, the damages can be devastating. The recent 2008 financial crisis is a major occurrence that proves the point.

Bloomfield Investment Corp. is the first Ivorian rating agency to emerge in French-speaking West Africa. In this market, the agency is quite beneficial for the regional ecosystem because due to geographical proximity, it has a better grasp of the economic, political and cultural environment. As a result, this *Made for Africa* organization closely follows the risk exposure of rated companies and also issues ratings on local currencies. Nevertheless, given the high level of corruption in the region, there is some skepticism regarding the quality of their company ratings and whether or not they are accurate. If you are yourself skeptical at this point, then you should throw this book away. It is an old cliché. A new generation of African companies has been established with good governance standards and practices and, as stated by the agency's CEO Stanislas Zeze, any hint of wrongdoing will jeopardize the credibility of Bloomfield Investment, its most important asset[17], which just cannot happen.

In the same financial area, *Made for Africa* companies in Senegal are making the private sector stronger and stronger. Teranga Capital, the first venture capital (VC) fund in the country, is one of them. The mission of Omar Cissé and Olivier Furdelle, the founders of Teranga Capital, is to finance SMEs, especially start-up businesses that operate in agriculture, poultry farming and horticulture, using a multisector strategy. In countries of the West and on a minor scale in South Africa, there are many VC and other funds compared to other regions of Africa. It is very important to support small local actors at the early stages of their development to help them become tomorrow's large companies. We are very optimistic about the future of Africa. Undoubtedly, developing a culture of competition will take Africa to the next level. Thus, the expansion of sources of financing also plays a key role in strengthening the private sector.

Expansion of sources of financing

The African Development Bank (2013) identifies two types of entrepreneurs in Africa: entrepreneurs motivated by necessity, in other words, individuals who are compelled to open a business because there are few viable alternatives available, and entrepreneurs motivated by opportunity. We will focus primarily on the first category, which represents 90% of the total number of entrepreneurs and constitutes the informal sector. The lack of financing from traditional institutions such as banks hinders the development of necessity entrepreneurs. In fact, the underground economy focuses on survival, with people looking to maximize profit on a very short-term basis – days, weeks and very rarely, months. They use almost no technology and no skilled labor. The consequences are heavy because the companies do not accumulate any resources to allow them to grow. Such a mindset also paralyzes the national economy. Profit maximization per se does not necessarily infer asset accumulation (Lautier, 2004). In order to give companies enough latitude to « think outside the box », they need more capital.

This set-up seems to be a chicken-and-egg problem. Why? Because in order to obtain bank loans, customers are required to meet an unreasonable number of conditions. This overly cautious behavior on the part of banks, combined with high interest rates (at least two digits), lead entrepreneurs to abandon their projects.
Philippe David (2009) points out that this behavior by commercial banks is not new in Africa. In the case of the Ivorian economy, the lack of financing prevented local agricultural ventures from expanding. Today, the development of various alternatives to traditional banks is a positive factor which fosters a more widespread culture of entrepreneurship in West Africa. Those new financial institutions act at different stages of African SME business cycles. First, microfinance represents a viable alternative to commercial banks in West Africa. After the implementation of the structural adjustment plans model, Africans saw this model as a genuine way to get out of a recession. And, to further develop microfinancing, the West African central bank established the PARMEC law[18] in 1993. This initiative gave former non-accredited cooperative unions the legitimacy to

collect savings while reassuring savers that their money was protected. In Ivory Coast, the COOPEC system, the longest established formal microfinancing institution, has granted credit to a large number of financially vulnerable small entrepreneurs and farmers to develop their activities. At the end of December 2006, there were about 116 cashiers/points of service, 660,279 customers, deposits totaling 65 billion FCFA (100 million euros) and about 26 billion FCFA (40 million euros) of credit issued. In 2007, the PARMEC act was reviewed, which increased the list of accredited institutions. In this context, new players emerged and supplemented the existing base, thus improving the funding environment for small business people. Money is lent more easily under more flexible conditions for projects in both rural and urban areas. Currently, when a business owner requests credit from a microfinancing institution, a team is assigned to the business. The team spends time with the owner and conducts a financial review (stream of cash flows, etc.) to assess the value of the company. At the end, two guarantors (or more depending on the business value) are required, who will undergo a similar screening process, and asked to use the business as collateral to raise the money. Through this process, potential customers can easily obtain between 7,000 and 15,000 euros. While that may seem like small sums, it still represents a starting point for the development of businesses. On this basis the Microcred group made numerous entrepreneurs happy since 2007 in Senegal, 2010 in Nigeria and 2011 in Ivory Coast, and the same is true for the Advans group since 2012 in Nigeria and Ivory Coast. These initiatives, combined with a decrease in small business taxes by West African governments, contribute to the formalization of SMEs, the «born again» SMEs.

Private equity, whose objective is not to lend money but rather to take equity stakes in companies, is another financing alternative for African SMEs. While this activity is not new in Africa, there have been increasingly more funds available to Africa over the last 10 years. One of the reasons why many private equity firms are emerging today is because of the impressive acquisition of pan-African telecommunications Celtel International BV in May 2005 by Mobile Telecommunications Co. (today Zain Group), a Kuwaiti group, for an amount of $3.4 billion USD. It highlighted a lot of potential for this industry. Since the term SME is quite broad, it should be pointed out that private equity firms are only looking for established SMEs, in particular those with the potential for high growth. Very small SMEs, such as those targeted by microfinance are good candidates for venture capital funds. Here, we do not use the term «start-up» to describe the target of VC, because in Africa there is no difference. The term «start-up» is a foreign expression which is quite fashionable at the moment and describes small SMEs. In addition to providing more funds, private equity entities provide management support to allow the acquired company to meet their growth objectives. Emerging Capital Partners (ECP) Investments is one of the industry leaders in Africa. As with pan-African Celtel, the fund supports many SMEs for a period of 4 to 6 years after a careful top-down analysis: first, based on the regions in which they operate, second, based on their sector of activities, such as telecommunications, financial services, education, etc. and finally, based on company profiles to see if there is a match with those of the fund targets (annual profits of at least 25%). Vincent Le Guennou, co-director of the fund, confirmed that both the demand in capital (less visible) and the offer of capital are on the rise in Africa[19]. In fact, the greatest demand for private equity is from pan-African companies. Nigeria, together with the entire West African region, represents the second largest investment area in Africa with some 28% of the total amount, just after South Africa[20].

More discreetly, crowdfunding is making its entrance on the continent and seems to be an evolution of African solidarity-based financing. In fact, «tontines» and other small informal traditional loan clubs are being replaced by the crowdfunding concept. A component of the sharing economy, crowdfunding is a form of financing for small-and-medium size projects, mostly innovative ones, by raising money from a large number of individuals through internet and digital platforms (Boyer, Chevalier, Léger , & Sannajust, 2016). Through donations (with or without reciprocity), loans and equity capital, this trendy model of funding gives immediate hope to small African entrepreneurs. The reason for this is because so far, most projects in Africa are financed thanks to its culture of solidarity. For example, there is an ingrained moral responsibility among Africans to help your wife's nephew fund his company based on one's status within the society… However, until now, there was no evidence that someone helped someone at a specific period with a set amount. Therefore, this advanced social tool is an evolution of African tradition, enabling donors to record their actions. We need to recognize that crowdfunding in Africa is still at an early stage. In 2015, there were about 19 digital platforms in Africa. We believe, however, that it will take a sizeable place as a source of funding for SMEs, as its evolution is tied to the acquisition of new technologies in Africa.

Acquisition of new technologies in Africa

The economic rise of West African countries, as forecast by their national development plans, has a great chance to be sustainable due to the important place dedicated to technology. At the beginning of his term, Nigerian president Muhammadu Buhari declared that vision 2020, which sees Nigeria among the top 20 economies in the world, will only be possible if science, technology and innovation are fully integrated into the economic national development process[21]. In terms of factors that have impacted globalization such as the expansion of the mobility of goods, people, products/services and capital, Maluquer de Motes believes that the most fundamental element of this process has been technology (2014). Today, major structural changes are taking place, including the reinforcement of submarine cables to better access the Internet and facilitate the shift to 4G Internet. Also, in order to fully take advantage of those changes, governments are sponsoring the establishment of infrastructures such as technology parks as well as using tax incentives to promote R&D and innovation. For drivers, this would represent better access to a network of roads and bridges. West Africa has been following in the footsteps of Silicon Valley in California, which features a large concentration of high-tech companies in the United States. In Lagos, there is the Yabacon Valley, in Grand Bassam (a UNESCO World Heritage site) there is the Information and Biotechnological Village of Technologies (VITIB) and in Dakar, there is the Cyber Village, which is expected to be replaced by the Diamniadio Digital Technology Park according to the Emerging Senegal Plan. Although those clusters are more recent than Silicon

Valley and do not have the same level of development, they still have similar characteristics: strong relationships with large corporations and investors (venture capitalists), access to high-speed Internet protected from power cuts, proximity to universities, flexible incubation conditions, and tax incentives. More and more, established African tech companies are moving to technology parks to combine their strengths with other companies. In September 2010, the Ivoirian group Weblogy, well known for its Abidjan.net platform, decided to relocate to Grand Bassam to take advantage of the Ivorian tech park. They repatriated most of their servers which until then were located in the U.S. More recently, at the beginning of 2015, the giant Africa Internet Group (AIG), the leader of e-commerce in Africa, transferred its offices to the Yabacon Valley. It is in the best interest of Africans to get involved in building such technology parks because in the long run, they will reap the benefits of the ecosystem, which could lead to a better organization of the lives of the people in West Africa.

1 – New technologies supporting political governance and communities

Supporting political governance

In order to maintain political stability in the West Africa region, governments have ventured into remarkably transparent initiatives. Based on regional historic facts, we note that the two major causes of political dissent are the legitimacy of heads of states and the management of public resources. To reduce the risk of fraud characterized by multiple voting, ballot box stuffing, and voter impersonation during the electoral process, Africans have decided to adopt biometric technology. In 2015, there were about 30 African countries among 55 using this technology, and experts forecast that it will be implemented in the entire continent by 2020. The power of biometrics occurs at many levels: when updating the electoral roll, when compiling the electoral roll with electoral kits, and during election day when validating biometrics data, an innovation in both Nigeria and Ivory Coast since 2015. In Nigeria, the Independent National Electoral Commission demonstrated its technological evolution during the last presidential election on April 28, 2015 with the introduction of permanent voter cards (PVCs) and card reader devices. The PVCs register authenticated information and then, on election day, digital fingerprints, which are almost impossible to counterfeit, are matched with data provided in the card. In Ivory Coast also, during the presidential election of October 25, 2015 the country's Independent Electoral Commission introduced something new – biometric fingerprint recognition using tabs. Those actions have increased the reliability of results and enlarged the national consensus shared by all the parties involved: political parties, populations and the international community. Communication is key during an election, so one of the electoral commission's main priorities is to provide information about the election process to make it fair for everyone. Commissions have always been active in this respect. They have expanded their communication channels, initially consisting of traditional media such as radio, TV, newspapers and posts, to include the Internet. The popularity of mobile phones, Internet and social media in Africa have driven those independent organizations to promote electoral web campaigns to reach a wider range of citizens within and outside country boundaries. For Mustapha Mbengue (2009), the electoral web consists of a set of Internet technologies that could contribute to greater involvement by citizens during the electoral process and debates. Facebook, Twitter, Blackberry Messenger, YouTube, Skype and other digital platforms have enabled the communication of educational information about the electoral process such as how it is conducted, opening and closing times of polling stations, and more broadly, it has given voters a chance to follow the election in real-time, from enrollment to election day.

In line with their strategy of increasing civic engagement during elections, commissions now target a new segment of potential voters mainly consisting of young people with access to the Internet from their smartphones through the use of apps. The number of Internet subscribers on smartphones keeps increasing and now represents 56% in Nigeria and 34% in Ivory Coast of the total number of mobile phone subscribers. There were many apps available during the most recent elections such as «Mon vote» in Ivory Coast and «My2015betterme» in Nigeria. In some cases, the app offered geolocation functionality to facilitate site identifications. In his approach to good governance, Marcel Banza (2015) highlights the important role that African civil societies play to reinforce democratic principles.

Indeed, Africans are using the web more and more for denouncing political wrongdoing. With the visibility and viral power that new technologies offer, the impact of those initiatives is huge. According to Senegalese digital expert Basile Niane[22] omitting to add the «E» (for electronic) before words like «democracy», «elections» and «citizens» shows an ignorance of modern Africa. During the last election, Nigerian civil society contributed to the general transparency effort using the theme of «electoral police» in talk-shows, online forums, and the creation of apps such as *Revoda*, initiated by the NGO Enough Is Enough Nigeria Coalition (EiE). During the 2012 presidential election in Senegal, the civil society was also very active on social media, as people were skeptical about outgoing President Abdoulaye Wade's «real» willingness to uphold democratic values. Web initiatives such as *SUNU 2012* and *Sama Baat* helped to raise Senegalese awareness about the electoral process and get citizens more involved. Generally speaking, the Internet and mobile phones are the roots of big changes in terms of the distribution of information. Indeed, even before the extensive use of social media during political elections, mobile phones were widespread. In the early 2000s, the innovative tool of the moment, a simple cellphone, enabled on site journalists to interact in real time with their home bases. This had an impact on the quality of radio and TV editorial content. With the social media revolution, Africans are now into participative democracy.

The second cause of dissent in West Africa is the management of public resources. To address this challenge, governments have adopted a model of electronic governance (e-governance) through a vast plan of modernizing state administrations, similar to what is being done abroad. This concept refers to the use of Internet technology as the platform for exchanging information, providing services and interacting with citizens, businesses, and other arms of government (Adeyemo, 2011). In the 2014 UN ranking on e-governance entitled «E-Government for the Future We

Want», we note some remarkable progress in West Africa in only two years: Nigeria moved up by 21 places and Senegal made a huge leap forward over 12 countries. E-governance boosts both the provision of daily services to citizens and better access (24/7) to public administration, a step that will help contain corruption at this level. Nigeria and Senegal are above the average in terms of e-governance for African nations, unlike Ivory Coast that has been working hard to catch up since 2004, considering its political problems over the past years, which have slowed down the process. According to the Ivorian minister of technology, the country is still on track to address this gap, mainly in three areas: the introduction of an unique ID number for all related administrative purposes, the total digitalization of the administrative system through a paperless approach, and the interconnection of various public organizations to compile all citizens' data; thus citizens will no longer be required to bring official documents such as birth certificates to prove their identity[23].In Nigeria, the teachers' e-registration in May 2006 marked the beginning of the digitalization of public administration. Today, there are about 11 targeted departments and we can now find the department of agriculture through «e-Agriculture». This online platform focused on agriculture had achieved an implementation rate of 80% in 2014 and represents an important promotional tool for agriculture. In Senegal, the E-Senegal vision emerged under the Wade administration. He allowed the country to develop efficient e-government tools, of which the best known is «servicepublic.gouv.sn», an online portal for administrative paperwork. It enables any citizen or company to complete more than 700 administrative tasks online. The tab «e-citoyen» is another original component of the platform that enables interactions with the Senegalese population. Very often, an opinion poll is organized to determine the most relevant issue among citizens, which is then addressed. The population can contribute ideas online and also sign petitions. As well, political leaders interact through social media to keep strengthening e-democracy. The central role played by social media during North Africa's 2011 Arab uprising, known as the *Arab Spring,* serves as a lesson: better be safe than sorry. Today, West Africa's governments use those platforms to really interact with their people and hear their complaints. Recently in Ivory Coast, a list of elements of national dissatisfaction compiled under the hashtag «#Les 200», is a good illustration of this. The government of Ivory Coast reacted promptly, cancelling the increase of electricity prices and the driver's license reform, both sources of dissatisfaction. This was a symbolic victory for democracy, for the Ivorian people, and for the African population. In the *Jeune Afrique* Magazine ranking (2016), Ivory Coast and Senegal now respectively rank second and third among 22 French-speaking countries.

Supporting the population

Innovation is at the center of the modernization of the economic and social environment in Africa. This is a milestone in terms of West Africa's development. Africans are now very active in electronic commerce (e-commerce), mobile commerce (m-commerce) and social commerce (s-commerce) to meet their needs. These new types of commerce, whose foundation rests on digital pillars such as online payments and promotions, definitely enable Africans to take part in a consumer society which is becoming more and more virtual. In his theory of consumption, French sociologist Jean Baudrillard (1970) points out that consumption, for all its complexity, remains essentially human and that «a growing society results from a set of compromises among equal democratic principles, which can be supported by the myth of abundance and well-being, and the critical imperative of upholding an order of privilege and domination». The added valued that digital solutions bring helps to reduce inequalities, in particular the gap between African consumers at the top level of Maslow's pyramid and those at the bottom, through a number of advantages accessible to all, such as transparency, speed, flexibility, and comparability to other desired products and services. It is difficult to estimate the size of the e-commerce market in West Africa, but generally, experts in Africa forecast that its value will reach $50 billion USD by 2018, a figure six times higher than in 2013[24]. Although still minor at the global level, the size of B2C e-commerce in Africa and its remarkable growth rate attracts foreign companies. Nigeria is without a doubt the e-commerce leader in West Africa. In 2012, the value of B2C e-commerce was estimated at $800 million USD. According to a 2015[25] study on consumer behavior done by start-up company Kaymu (now JumiaMarket), the city of Lagos represents the largest potential market in the country. The Konga and Jumia (AIG group) online shopping platforms reflect the boom of e-commerce in Nigeria. In March 2013, they claimed to deliver at least 1,000 orders a day [26] together, an impressive result, as some experts had forecast the failure of the adoption of such a new model in Africa due to obvious challenges regarding online payment and delivery services. Mobile represents the first of the Key Success Factors (KSF) of African e-commerce. Behind only Asia, Africa is the second largest market in terms of the development of mobile phones. Indeed, more people access the Internet using cell phones. Kaymu highlighted that 69% of its traffic is coming from smartphones, and 31% from computers. Given that only a small part of the population has a bank account, it may appear as an obstacle when it comes to selling products online. However, African e-sellers have adapted well to local situations by offering more payment options compared to what is available in industrialized countries. This represents the second KSF of e-commerce in Africa, because it allows all social classes to take part in the ecosystem, while at the same removing anxiety from payment card holders afraid to be scammed due to the high rate of banking fraud. Additionally, the 2016 ranking of countries on B2C e-commerce issued by the UNCTAD [27] reflects the constant improvement of factors fostering the development of e-commerce in the region. The terrific progress of Senegal which climbed by 21 places in two years, Nigeria's excellent ranking and the first appearance of Ivory Coast in the ranking demonstrate this. Finally, the last KSF of e-commerce in West Africa is delivery. In contrast to online companies operating in developed countries that outsource all shipping, African start-ups have control of all the supply chain process to ensure customer satisfaction. In 2015, of its total visits, the JumiaMarket platform registered 55% of returning visitors. Although many factors come into play for gaining customer loyalty, such as price and platform reputation, companies could never have achieved this result without fully covering the entire supply chain, as the delivery service market is not well developed in the above-mentioned countries. When it comes to shipping a package to the countryside, however, e-sellers outsource delivery to outside transportation companies.

Since the implementation of structural adjustment plans, national development projects such as electrification have been curtailed. Today, thanks to new technologies, solar energy seems a viable and cheap resource to use. West Africa benefits from exceptional sunshine estimated on average between 5 and 7 kWh/m2/per day, about twice the amount of sunshine in France[28]. French businessman Vincent Bollore predicts that the development of solar energy will be similar to that of the mobile phone[29]. Nigeria is one of the West African countries that suffers the most from a shortage of power. As demographic and economic factors are both on the rise, there is a general increase of household consumption. Nigerian society is becoming increasingly more sophisticated and as a result, people are using electric home appliances, which consume a lot of electricity. In this regard, residential electricity consumption accounts for 58% of the country's total consumption[30].To overcome shortages of electricity and power outages, companies and people use generators, as mentioned earlier. However, generators are far from eco-friendly, and thus a social crisis is leading to an environmental crisis...

Thanks to the efforts of the private sector, an original concept has emerged that seems to be a viable solution to improve Nigerian living conditions – mobile electricity. The telecom company MTN, together with Nova Lumos, a leader in the distribution of solar equipment, launched «MTN-Lumos solar solution» in 2014, a solar kit that brings light to thousands of families in Nigeria, particularly those living in rural areas. Based on a pay-as-you-go concept, which is in fact a prepaid solution, users adapt their consumption according to their needs and budget. Another benefit of the development of new technologies, along with increased use of the Internet due to its cheaper cost, has enabled telemedicine to emerge. Telemedicine is the remote delivery of healthcare services. It is generally managed from city centers to help small town residents using various technological supports such as videoconferencing apps. The concept of telemedicine appears to be a reliable way of increasing the life expectancy of Africans because it gives medical access to a part of the population so far excluded from decent healthcare services. In contrast to developed countries where patients who have online medical consultations often do so because of time constraints, patients in Africa who are getting treatments using remote medicine have no other alternatives. Governments are not building enough fully equipped medical facilities in small towns due to budget constraints and invite patients to go to nearby larger cities to be attended by doctors. Therefore, online consultations, remote ultrasounds, and online medical teaching are examples of how digital technology can help people at little cost while waiting for the government to act. The Senegalese «Assistance médico-chirurgicale et Télémédecine» campaign initiated by the AMREF in 2011 illustrates this point[31]. A telemedicine platform has been established connecting two public hospitals in the capital of Dakar with four regional centers covering the areas of Ziguinchor, Kolda, Sedhiou, Tambacounda, Louga, Matam and Thies. As a result of this initiative, it was estimated in 2014 that a least 2,302 patients had had consultations and received treatment afterwards, 1,158 patients had had surgery and 211 people received proper medical training.

Today, the new way of life in Western societies is structured on the sharing economy concept. Backed by new technologies, the sharing economy reshapes the current model of capitalism that encourages ownership of goods to an alternative approach that instead, promotes a crowd-based capitalism (Sundararajan, 2016). The added value of this concept is the optimization of individual surplus resources. NYU professor Arun Sundararajan considers that the rise of this type of economy represents in some ways a step back to the era prior to the Industrial Revolution. He is absolutely right. However, without going that far back in time, we can look at the current way of life in Africa to observe similarities. Indeed, this way of thinking based on the principle of sharing is in the African DNA. For Edem Kodjo (1985), the former president of the Organization of African Unity (now the African Union), the African mentality, derived from the complexity of the world's structure, is apprehensive about scientific research, technical development and management of geographical areas, a view that is not necessarily shared in so-called modern societies. With such high poverty rates in different parts of the continent, if Africans had not adopted the value of sharing, where would Africa be today in terms of transportation, housing, etc.? Nigerians, Ivoirians and Senegalese pool their efforts to move forward. However, their traditional sharing economy must evolve to the modern one to integrate technology, in particular Information Systems (IS). IS collects, stores, processes data and also enables «peer to peer» interactions between people. With respect to African agriculture, we mentioned earlier the lack of mechanization in farms as a major cause of low productivity and the use of child labor. Based on a collaborative consumption model, the start-up

Hello Tractor adds an IT dimension to the traditional African sharing economy that enables farmers to get access to affordable tractors. What makes *Hello Tractor* collaborative is the innovative feature that helps find nearby tractors equipped with a GPS antenna to rent them out to farmers who need them for a period of time. The transaction is completed through mobile money transfers. The «smart» tractors are able to complete work in 8 hours that would have taken a farmer with a machete 40 days[32] to complete. For an investment of $4,500 USD, a Nigerian farmer can boost his productivity and also make money when not using his tractor. This is but one example that through small, funded initiatives, $60,000 USD in the case of Hello Tractor, start-ups are able to reduce wealth inequality on the continent. In addition to the agricultural sector, start-ups are taking control of the online entertainment ecosystem in West Africa.

2 – West Africa online interactions

West Africa, along with the Sub-Saharan region, has the world's youngest population[33]. Creative initiatives are necessary to keep these young people occupied. Thus, many entertaining activities are organized for them by both public and private organizations: concerts, fairs, exhibitions, sports activities, etc. However, nothing seems more powerful than the Web 2.0 and its ramifications that have been emerging since the early 2000s and continue to expand. Today, social media is the center of interest of young Africans and it also represents a means of combat. African youths are interacting online in the same way as their Asian, American and European peers to enjoy the benefits of having learning, entertainment, relatives and friends, spiritual guides and others at hand. Facebook is the most popular social media network in Africa with 129 million users in 2016 and its penetration rate keeps increasing in the region. According to *We are social,* in January 2016 there were about 1.8 million active users respectively in Ivory Coast and Senegal, and 15 million in Nigeria. If we take a closer look at Nigeria, we can see that there was an increase of about 34% in the number of users in only two years (2014-2016). Also, not surprisingly, young people age 20 to 30 account for 46% of the total online population. In the online world, platforms such as blogs, forums, and social media make interaction accessible and valuable to users. Their structure is organized around three functions: pull, facilitate and match (Parker, Van Alstyne, & Choudary, 2016). Generating traffic is the first challenge of a web administrator. The number of visits to *Abidjan.net* (Weblogy Group), the largest Ivorian news platform, experienced a peak for the first time during the country's military coup in 1999. Through its chat boxes and the display of real-time news feeds, resident Ivoirians and those abroad could get information about the development of the crisis while the state television was silent. Before that, people had to make making numerous phone calls to get information. Beyond the cost savings of telecommunications, *Abidjan.net* has revolutionized the Internet in Ivory Coast as its co-founder Jil-Alexandre N'Dia explains, because the platform enables people to be «closer»[34]. Once there is enough traffic on your platform, the user experience should be optimized. In this regard, there is no golden rule except that the interface should be user-friendly. When we look at the ergonomics of the *Carmudi Nigeria* website, for example, we notice that it is very easy to select a vehicle due to good sort and filter options that help remove non-desired fields. This platform has won the 2015 Beacon of ICT Awards as the automobile portal of the year and also for contributing to the development of new technologies in the country[35]. The last main objective of a web platform is to match people. Friendite, Abidjan-loves or RencontreSenegal are local start-ups that make online dating possible through their platform. Users can interact on live chat boxes with many features, including cameras. Some lucky people find their soul mate this way. It is a true revolution of African traditions in terms of love and romance, which are usually hidden from families until the day of the marriage proposal. If one of the three main functions of a platform fails to deliver properly, we immediately face a negative network effect which may cause the platform to disappear in the long run[36]. In the case of dating websites, misleading profiles is one of the main causes of negative network effects because users cannot connect with the «right person». This is a tool used by cyber-crooks who are quite active in West Africa, particularly in Nigeria and Ivory Coast. Even though data from the Crime Complaint Center[37] show that online blackmail is a global phenomenon, consequences are felt much more strongly in developing countries. As Jean-Jacques Bogui (2010) points out, repercussions ensue on three fronts – economic, education and image. However, efforts made by both the Nigerian Police Special Fraud Unit and the Ivorian unit fighting against cybercrimes (PLCC) have helped to contain its development. According to the PLCC, in 2014, the rate of sextortion in Ivory Coast decreased by 54%[38]. In the early 2000s, Nigeria's image was strongly associated with a negative image stemming from what Nigerians call «419 scams» – mail scams, lottery scams, etc. Today, the country's image is being associated with wealth, power, Nollywood, quite a quite seductive image that currently makes Nigeria one of the best places to invest in the world.

Online platforms are more or less a reflection of the traditional ecosystem in which we live. This is the reason why it is no surprise to see both public and private institutions interacting on them since they follow the crowd. However, the power given to civil society thanks to the Internet through influencers, bloggers, and the like is a real consolidation of freedom of speech in a continent known for its absence. They can make their voices heard through viral campaigns with no intervention by the police. We do not intend to portray a continent in which freedom of speech is the most valued privilege, however. People are also looking for entertainment. Over the past decade, we have witnessed the expansion of African entertainment on the web. In the case of public institutions, African state TV networks take advantage of the opportunity to make themselves known internationally. Three years ago, the Ivory Coast national TV station *Radio Télévision Ivoirienne (RTI)* started using a digital strategy that includes a presence on social media, the development of «RTI Mobile» apps and streaming broadcasts available on both computers and mobiles. At the end of 2014, the RTI group was divided into two parts: an entity focused on production for better quality programs, and the other focused on distribution, which invests in movies and then sells them. As a result, we note with great satisfaction that on February 15, 2016, the RTI Facebook account crossed the symbolic threshold of one million subscribers. On June 6, 2016, its YouTube channel reported a total of 34,542 subscribers and more than 17 million views. Those good performances, according to Pierre Barrot[39], highlight the adaptation of African media to the evolution of demand. In the old days, African consumers were looking for foreign content, whereas today they choose «made in Africa» productions as a result of the impact of Nollywood in the western region. Along with public organizations, numerous private companies are developing the online entertainment industry. In Nigeria, entertainment represented a $4 billion USD industry in 2014, which is expected to double by 2019[40]. Since 2011, the online platform *iROKO TV*, also called the «African Netflix» has revolutionized the Nollywood movie distribution because of its high quality productions. In fact, one of the success factors of the Nigerian *home video* is its distribution network. In the traditional network, the sales channel, also known as the «marketers», need to sell their stock of original DVDs very quickly before pirated versions start to be sold on the market. This approach had the merit of enabling both the distribution of series and movies and minimizing losses generated by piracy. However, with the advent of digital technology, distribution needed to be leveraged. This is the shift in demand caused by the rapid development of social media that gave an opportunity to Jason Njoku, founder of *iROKO TV*, to transform Nollywood into a digital industry. Online TV allows Africans, regardless of their location, to enjoy programs any time. Another good example of online TV in Senegal is *Yamatele,* which is more focused on the streaming of TV shows and series. The «Carrapide» group, to which *Yamatele* belongs, refers to a popular means of public transportation in Senegal, a small, inexpensive bus known for its colorful appearance. With 2,336 subscribers in June 2016, this platform reflects daily life in Senegal on a micro level. More broadly, those initiatives, stimulated by both public and private institutions, contribute to the development and influence of African culture in the world.

The online entertainment ecosystem is completed by individuals whose nicknames depend on their sphere of influence: Facebookers, youtubers, etc. Their popularity can be measured through their numbers of friends, followers or views generated by their posts. For the first time in West Africa, all the key influencers of the region were gathered in Dakar from June 3-5 to discuss how to promote African digital productions. The organization of the event, the «Festival d'Afrique des Blogueurs et Youtubeurs» is commendable and demonstrates that Africans are building the foundations for the development of web activities. Not only does the expansion of online activities create jobs as increasingly more community managers are hired, but it also gives higher visibility to African traditions. For example, Touba is the second largest city in Senegal and the holy city of the Mourid Brotherhood. With a population of more than one million, this city is well known for its high concentration of marabouts, which are «special» Muslim spiritual guides. They are special because they are truly geniuses, going beyond the spiritual aspect to assist business owners in the development of their companies. Without knowing the Mourides in depth, we can say that this brotherhood has set up rules of conduct for its members, who are considered disciples or «taalibe», and must obey their marabouts in return for their protection and that of their business. Marabouts have always used technology to expand their community – from 1991, when the first computer arrived in Touba, to March 1996, when Senegal was officially connected to Internet, until now with the advent of social media. Computers have helped marabouts to build a database to better manage their clients/disciples, and to teach foreign languages, especially Arabic, among other things. Today, they use computers to reach clients online, as some have their own website, while others give online consultations through Skype. They maintain a close relationship with their clients on Facebook and Twitter and also on professional social media platforms such as Viadeo and LinkedIn. With more than 467 million users on LinkedIn in 2017, the world seems to have no borders for the marabouts. In fact, they exploit what Small & Vorgan (2009) call an artificial sense of intimacy to grow their network. Also, marabouts are quite open-minded and resilient to change, as Liliane Kuczynski (2013) explains in her description of the strategy of visibility used in Paris by West African marabouts. Indeed, after being acclimatized to the French lifestyle in the 1960s, marabouts coming from Muslim West African countries such as Senegal, Mali and Guinea, changed their offer to appeal to new clients looking for exoticism. First, they understood that it was vital to change their environment, i.e. leave migrant facilities assigned to them to live in better places, in areas decent enough to attract their new clients. They then changed their title of «marabout» to more familiar ones among Europeans, such as psychic, psychologist, or clairvoyant. This helped them to be cost effective because instead of creating a new market, they entered an existing market by adding a «new» offering. Following this, they adapted their working practices to meet those of the local industry, giving «consultations» and «prescriptions» as their peer practitioners do. In terms of marketing, along with word-of-mouth, they started advertising in French newspapers such as *Liberation* in 1984-1985, on the radio, and distributing flyers at central locations such as metro stations. The adaptability displayed by Mourid marabouts is similar to that of African government leaders, which makes us believe that Nigeria, Ivory Coast and Senegal are the next emerging countries.

The next emerging countries

1 – Nigeria and the MINT countries

Mexico, Indonesia, Nigeria and Turkey form a new emerging economic group known as the MINT countries. The size of their population, their strategic location and their high growth rate are characteristics that make them quite attractive to the world. Since 2013, they are viewed as the replacement to the BRICS group which is at the moment on a relative downturn.

On October 23, 2015, as Goldman Sachs closed its BRICS fund after years of poor returns to merge with a broader emerging-market fund, it symbolically reflected the end of an era and a beginning of another, a view supported by the economist Jim O'Neill, who created the BRIC acronym and now the MINT acronym. This brings strong credibility toward the MINT countries' sustainable development. Brazil, which under the Lula administration seemed on a good track to prosperity, is now experiencing a decrease of domestic demand, as well as a series of unprecedented strikes and protests. In Russia, the situation is quite similar in some ways. Because of its annexation of Crimea, the country is suffering from important economic sanctions from the U.S. and the European Union. The situation worsened with the collapse of oil prices, plunging Russia into an unprecedented nightmare. In the case of China, its growth rate decreased from 7.3% in 2014 to 6.9% in 2015. Some experts, such as French professor emeritus of economics Michel Aglietta, see the risk of this downturn spreading to other countries of the world. Africa in particular will suffer, as China is quite «seductive» to the continent. India, for its part, represents the best student in the class, with an expected growth rate of 7.8% in 2016, embedded in a context of demographic increase. South Africa is a victim of the domino effect engendered by the contraction of the demand for raw materials from some of the other members of the group, especially China. Its growth rate in 2016 is not expected to reach more than 1.4%.

As a result of the decline, South Africa has lost its economic leadership in Africa, something that has generated more interest in Nigeria. This would help Nigeria reach its long-term objective under the national development plan Vision2020. Indeed, for 2020, the plan forecasts the growth rate of the Nigerian economy to reach 13.8%, supported by both the agricultural and manufacturing sectors. This is a strong and fast expansion that Nigeria is aiming at, and will then turn it into a fair development. Nigeria's potential to become an emerging country therefore includes an economic dimension along with those related to the institutional order and the environment. Ivory Coast also aims for the 2020 time frame to expand its development.

2 – Ivory Coast

The key strategic thrusts for the country are centered around four main phases: accelerating the structural transformation of the economy through industrialization, developing infrastructure, enhancing institution and governance performance, and accelerating the development of human capital and social welfare.

In the eyes of Ivorian authorities, the structural transformation of the economy is crucial for meeting the 2020 objective. This will be possible through a diversification strategy which takes into consideration improvements in the quality of products, particularly agricultural ones, industrial activities, and leveraging the potential for its services activities.

Infrastructure development will also be carried out, which will increase the overall economic development process. As we saw in the previously described example of Snedai, this process is proceeding at an intensive pace. In addition, the implementation of factories in Abidjan and large road and bridge construction sites are tangible signs that demonstrate the willingness of the authorities to fulfill their commitment. The high growth rate in Ivory Coast is also an indicator of its potential for becoming an emerging country.

In the case of Senegal, its economic growth rate has been close to that of its population growth rate for more than a decade.

3 – Senegal

In contrast to the previous countries, Senegal aims for the 2035 time frame, when a new Senegal should emerge to embrace a solidarity economy under a strict rule of law.

To achieve this goal, the Emerging Senegal Plan focuses on three main areas:
- A substantial transformation of the economy and the development of sectors that create wealth and generate jobs;
- An improvement in living conditions and a stronger fight against social inequalities;

- A reinforcement of security, stability, governance and the protection of individual rights and freedoms.

Regarding this last point, it is important to point out that Senegal is the only country of the WAEMU area (West African Economic and Monetary Union) that has never experienced a military coup in its history.

These three strategic thrusts, according to the Senegalese authorities, should create great conditions for significant economic growth as a result of their synergies, leading it to the status of emerging country.

The vision, however, can only take shape if energy production and business climate problems are resolved, supported by a more robust human capital.

Conclusion

Africa is the continent of the future. This is the main takeaway of this document, based on the sample overview of three countries, as well as related explanations and examples.

From this general presentation, we can be optimistic about the development of technologies and the commitment of country leaders to leverage the numerous assets that Africa possesses into an engine of unprecedented economic growth.

Only a few of these assets have been presented here. Many more raw materials could have been included in our description of Africa's rich reservoir of assets, but those that have been highlighted are enough to get the message across, i.e. that Africa needs to manufacture its own products instead of exporting raw materials and waiting for others to process them and ship them back as refined products, which in the end do not really meet the real needs of its countries. If Africa succeeds in doing this, the entire continent will be emerging.

Nigeria, Ivory Coast and Senegal are definitively the three next emerging countries because they are located at the right place, both their business and political leaders are following the right strategy, and more importantly, at the right time. Unless the access to financing gets restricted, nothing else would prevent these countries from meeting their objectives. Africa as a whole has the support of the African Development Bank, a continental financial institution. The three countries also have access to their own capital markets. Furthermore, Ivory Coast and Senegal operate within a common area consisting of eight countries (Benin, Burkina Faso, Guinea-Bissau, Ivory Coast, Mali, Niger, Senegal, Togo) to mobilize necessary funds.

Endnotes

Preface

[1] Those are small savings plans carried out for most part by market woman traders where they put in common their profit in order to finance an investment for either a private or a collective interest. The loan system is commonly called « Ajo » or « Esusu » in Nigeria and « tontine » in Ivory Coast and Senegal

First part

[1] Richard Florida, The Rise of Creative Class (revisited), 2014

[2] It refers to the boom of US the oil and natural gas productions since 2010 due to technological advancements, a modern combination of horizontal drilling and hydraulic fracturing. As a result of this revolution, the US is less dependant on oil imports from OPEC countries

[3] Moustapha Kassé, L'économie du Sénégal, p 90-91

[4] Called in Ivory Coast « Caisse de stabilisation », this institution aimed to contain volatility in prices of the country commodities

[5] Leon Naka, Le tiers-monde et la crise d'endettement des années 80 – Fléchissement des flux financiers en direction des pays en développement, 1989, p. 59-60

[6] Aliou Ngamby Ndiaye, Les Chiffres du Tourisme au Sénégal, 15/02/14 – SENEPLUS Économie –

[7] L'observatoire de l'Afrique de l'Ouest n°6, p 19, Avril 2015

[8] A literary and political movement born in the late 1930s linked to anti-colonial sentiment and whose emblematic figures are Aime Césaire and Leopold Sedar Senghor

[9] John Igué, L'Afrique de l'Ouest: entre espace, pouvoir et société. Une géographie de l'incertitude, 2006, p 179

[10] KPMG, Infrastructure 100 World Markets Report, p. 7/55, 2014

[11] Physical interview with him on 06/18/16, Madrid, Spain

[12] The Hofstede Centre, www.geert-hofstede.com

[13] Gwenaëlle Ogandaga, Le respect de l'âge comme caractéristique du management des hommes : existe-t-il un modèle africain de GRH, Document de travail du LEM 2007-22, lem.icl lille.fr/Portals/2/actus/DP_200722.pdf

[14] This designation, developed by African economist and author Samir Amin, refers to western capitals and agglomerations

[15] Pierre Barrot, Nollywood: Le phénomène vidéo au Nigéria, 2005, p. 52

[16] www.projectactnollywood.com.ng/about

Second part

[1] Those are countries which are less developed than the semi-periphery and core countries, respectively developing and industrialized countries

[2] Data from CEDEAO - www.ecowas.int -

[3] At the *Africa CEO Forum* in Abidjan, March 21-22 2016

[4] XIVe International convention of educational cities, Rosaria 2016, in Argentina

[5] From 1895 until 1960, a group of eight French colonial territories in Africa formed a federation known as the French West Africa, consisting of Mauritania, Senegal, French Sudan (now Mali), French Guinea, Ivory Coast, Upper Volta (now Burkina Faso), Dahomey (now Benin) and Niger

[6] An interprofessional Labor Movement Union

[7] In reference to the ideological separation between the ultra-nationalist leaders like Sekou Toure and those who opted for liberalization. Declaration in June 1978 to Radio-Canada

[8] África no sueña con Europa, *Mundo Negro* n°616 – Mayo 2016

[9] Amount necessary for an illegal crossing from Senegal to Spain. Investigation : L'appel de l'Europe des Sénégalais, envers et contre tout; Christophe Châtelot, *Le Monde*, 11/09/15

[10] Agreement A/P1/5/79 on May 29th 1979 from the Economic Community of West African States about the free movement of people

[11] Akwaba'n Work, Influence avec Stanislas Zézé – Bloomfield – 03/16/16 – YouTube

[12] Ecobank, Middle Africa Insight Series / Energy / Nigeria, Outlook for Nigerian downstream market, chart 1 – Fuel subsidies paid by Nigeria's government 2006 – 2015e $ billion, 27 July 2015

[13] Stakeholder Democracy Network, Nigeria's fuel subsidy, August 2015, p. 13

[14] Elisha Bala-Gbogbo, Africa's Richest Man Will Fix Nigeria's Chronic Fuel Crisis, 01/13/16 – Bloomberg –

[15] Maureen Grisot, Nigéria : pourquoi le premier producteur africain de pétrole manque d'essence, 22/05/12 – *Le Monde*

[16] Mbuyi Kabunda Badi, Crecimiento y desarrollo, ¿Buenos vecinos en África?, *Mundo Negro* n°616, 05/16, p. 34

[17] Lors d'une interview réalisée par Christian Jarrin pour le compte du journal *AllPeopleFrom*. Publication le 02/10/2014

[18] Projet d'appui à la réglementation des mutuelles d'épargne et de crédit

[19] Grand invité Éco d'ici Éco d'ailleurs, Vincent Le Guennou 1re partie – RFI

[20] Club Afrique de l'AFIC, Le Livre Blanc du Capital-Investissement, 05/04/16, p. 20

[21] At the National Research and Innovation Council meeting held on January 7, 2016 in Abuja

[22] Basile Niane's vision on the use of the web for the 2012 election in Senegal. Aboubacar Sadikh N'Diaye, Livre Blanc Présidentielle 2.0: Facebook, Twitter et autres réseaux sociaux pour les élections 2012, p. 81

[23] Seminar on the development of e-government in Abidjan last December 7, 2015 - www.telecom.gouv.ci

[24] International Trade Centre 2015

[25] Kaymu, E-Commerce in Nigeria : Market trends and consumer behavior, 2015

[26] Oxford Business Group, The Report Nigeria 2013, p. 221

[27] The United Nations Conference on Trade and Development – www.unctad.org

[28] Les Connaissances des Énergies, Mix énergétique de l'Afrique de l'Ouest, 2016 - www.connaissancedesenergies.org

[29] In an interview conducted by Thierry Fabre on behalf of the magazine *Challenges*. Published on 01/13/2016

[30] GIZ, 2nd edition, June 2015 report « The Nigerian Energy Sector », p. 37

[31] L'AMREF Flying Doctors is considered the largest public health NGO in Africa. Established in 1957, the NGO is based in 30 countries and jointly leads more than 150 programs to help the most remote populations in Africa

[32] Jim Dallke, Meet the Guys From Hello Tractor, the Company that Looks to Revolutionize Farming in Nigeria, 6/3/14 – ChicagoInno –

[33] Publication of the *GlobalPost* on 10/08/14 about the median age per country. It shows that there are 1.2 billion people aged 15 to 24 years. In the ranking of countries with the largest number of populations, Africa gets the top 15 places. The median age in Nigeria is 18.2, in Côte d'Ivoire 20.3 and in Senegal 18.4

[34] In an interview by Africa 24 on 08/07/14 "The Meet of Africa 24" during the US-Africa summit in Washington

[35] It is one of the most prestigious events of the tech industry in Nigeria, organized by *Nigeria Communications Week* since 2008

[36] The *Network effects* refer to the impact that the number of users of a platform has on the value created for each user. When this network effect is negative, increasing the number of users can reduce the value created for each user (Parker, Van Alstyne et Choudary 2016, p. 17)

[37] It is an organization specialized in the collection of offenses committed through the Internet, in partnership with the FBI - www.ic3.gov

[38] Annual report 2014, DITT – Scientific Police Cote d'Ivoire, p. 4 – http://cybercrime.interieur.gouv.ci/?q=rapports-dactivités

[39] Interview by François Mazet on behalf of the RFI channel, December 27, 2015 – www.rfi.fr

[40] PWC, Entertainment and media outlook 2015-2019 South Africa – Nigeria – Kenya, 6th annual

Bibliography

Adeyemo, A. (2011, January). E-government implementation in Nigeria : An assessment of Nigeria's global e-gov ranking. *Academic Journals, 2*(1), 11-19.

African Development Bank. (2014). *African Development Report 2014 : Regional Integration for Inclusive Growth.* Abidjan.

Amin, S., Diouf, M., Founou-Tchuigoua, B., Zita, L., & Ndiaye, A. (2005). *Afrique exclusion programmée ou renaissance ? : Forum du Tiers Monde Forum Mondial des Alternatives.* Paris: Maisonneuve & Larose.

AMREF Flying Doctors. (n.d.). *Rapport d'activité 2014.*

Atsain, N. (2015, April). Migration <<capital économique>> des migrants en Afrique de l'ouest: le cas des migrants Burkinabé en Côte d'Ivoire. *European Scientific Journal, 11*(10), 340-353.

Autorité de Regulation des Télécommunications/Tic de Côte d'Ivoire. (2016). *Données statistiques annuelles du secteur des télécommunications - 2015.*

Banque Africaine de Développement. (2013). Chapitre 4: Le financement du secteur privé. In *Rapport sur le développement en Afrique 2011* (pp. 91-112).

Banque Africaine de Développement. (2013). *Rapport sur le developpement en Afrique 2011 - Chapitre 6 Développement de l'entrepreneuriat.*

Banque Africaine de Développement. (2015, Avril). *L'Observatoire de l'Afrique de l'Ouest.*

Banque Mondiale. (2015, Décembre 18). Les migrations internationales atteignent un niveau record.

Banza, M. (2015). *Participación popular y buena gobernanza en África: Balance y perspectivas para 2063*. Madrid: Los libros de la Catarata.
Barrot, P., Oladunjoye, T., Noy, F., Abdoulaye, I., Fuita, F., Lumisa, G., . . . Harding, F. (2005). *Nollywood : Le phénomène vidéo au Nigéria*. Paris: L'Harmattan.
Baudrillard, J. (1970). *La société de consommation* (Folio essais - Gallimard ed.). Editions Denoël.
BBC. (2014, January 6). The MINT countries : Next economic giants ? *BBC News Magazine*.
BCEAO. (2014). *Note d'information 4ème trimestre 2014*. Banque Centrale des Etats de l'Afrique de l'Ouest, Dakar.
Besada, H., Tok, E., & Winters, K. (2013, March). South Africa in the BRICS : Opportunities, Challenges and Prospects. *AFRICA INSIGHT, 42*(4).
Beugré, C. (2004). HRM in Ivory Coast. In K. Kamoche, Y. Debrah, F. Horwitz, & G. Muuka, *Managing Human Resources in Africa*. Routledge.
Beuret, M., & Michel, S. (2008). *La Chinafrique : Pékin à la conquête du continent noir*. Paris: Grasset.
Bogui, J.-J. (2010). La cybercriminalité, menace pour le développement : Les escroqueries internet en Côte d'Ivoire. *Afrique Contemporaine, 2*(234).
Bolzman, C., Gakuba, T.-O., & Guissé, I. (2011). *Migrations des jeunes d'Afrique subsaharienne: Quels défis pour l'avenir ?* Paris: L'Harmattan.
Boyer, K., Chevalier, A., Léger, J.-Y., & Sannajust, A. (2016). *Le crowdfunding*. Paris.
Centre de Recherche Politique d'Abidjan. (2015). La tablette biométrique ou innovation technologique : limites et possibilités. *Election présidentielle d'octobre 2015 en Côte d'Ivoire :*

Quels enseignements pour la consolidation de la démocratie ? Abidjan.

Cessou, S. (2015, Octobre-Novembre). Afrique, enfer et eldorado. *Manière de voir - Le Monde Diplomatique*(n°143).

CLUB AFRIQUE DE L'AFIC. (2016). *Le livre Blanc du capital-investissement en Afrique: Pour renforcer le tissu entrepreneurial en Afrique.*

CNUCED. (2015). *Le développement économique en Afrique Rapport 2015.* Conférence des Nations Unies sur le Commerce Et Développement.

Comité Technique du RGPH. (2014). *Recensement Général de la Population et de l'habitat 2014: Principaux résultats préliminaires.*

David, P. (2009). *La Côte d'Ivoire.* Paris: Editions KARTHALA.

De Montclos, M.-A. (1994). *Le Nigéria.* Paris: Editions KARTHALA.

Diop, M.-C. (2002). *Le Sénégal à l'heure de l'information : Technologies et société.* Paris: Editions KARTHALA.

Dubois, J. (2016, Janvier 28). La Chine provoquera-t-elle une crise économique mondiale en 2016 ? *LE HUFFINGTON POST.*

Dubresson, A., & Raison, J.-P. (2003). *L'Afrique subsaharienne : Une géographie du changement.* Paris: Armand Colin.

Duhem, V. (2016, Mai 2). Côte d'Ivoire : les annonces d'Alassane Ouattara pour calmer la grogne sociale. *Jeune Afrique.*

Dumont, R. (1962). *L'Afrique noire est mal partie* (Nouvelle édition octobre 2012 ed.). Paris: Editions du Seuil.

Economic Community of West African States (ECOWAS). (n.d.). *Trade*. Retrieved from ECOWAS: www.ecowas.int/ecowas-sectors/trade/
EFInA. (2014). *EFInA Access to Financial Services in Nigeria 2014 Survey : Key Findings*.
Enquête Exclusive M6. (2015, Avril 12). Milliardaires du pétrole, bidonvilles et gratte-ciels : l'incroyable visage du Nigéria. France.
Florio, L. (2016, Enero 07). Ocho claves del Banco Mundial sobre el rumbo de la economia en 2016. *LA VANGUARDIA*.
Forest, C. (2011). L'industrie du cinéma en Afrique. *Afrique Contemporaine*(n°238).
Godet, A., Olivier, M., & Kibangula, T. (2016, Avril 21). Vos ministres sont-ils actifs sur les réseaux sociaux ? *Jeune Afrique*.
Hart, K. (1973, March). Informal Income Opportunities and Urban Employment in Ghana. *The Journal of Modern African Studies, 11*(1), 61-89.
Igué, J. (2006). *L'Afrique de l'Ouest: entre espace, pouvoir et société. Une géographie de l'incertitude*. Karthala.
IMF. (2016, June). Runaway SUCCESS: Nigeria's film industry is taking off. *Finance & Development, 53*(2), 30-32.
International Trade Centre. (2015). International E-Commerce in Africa : The Way Forward.
Kabunda, M., & (Cord.). (2011). *Africa y la cooperacion con el Sur desde el Sur*. Madrid: Los Libros De La Catarata.
Kerdoudi, J. (2015). *Printemps ou hiver arabe ?* Paris: l'Harmattan.
Kodjo, E. (1985). *... et demain l'Afrique*. Paris: Editions Stock.

Kuczynski, L. (2013, Décembre 05). *Les marabouts ouest-africains à Paris: occupation spatiale, stratégies de visibilité et ouverture sur l'imaginaire.* HAL.

Laboratoire SEDET/CNRS. (n.d.). *Fiche Resumée Africapolis : Dynamiques de l'urbanisation ouest-africaine 1950-2020.* Retrieved from Agence Française de Développement: www.afd.fr/webdav/site/afd/shared/PUBLICATIONS/THEMATIQUES/autres-publications/BT/0808ProjetFicheResumeeAfricapolisV4.pdf

Lanneau, G., & Scarlett, A. (2013). *Le bien-être des migrants en Afrique de l'ouest : Etude de cas de quatre pays d'accueil dans la région.* Organisation Internationale pour les Migrations (OIM), Genève.

Lautier, B. (2004). *L'économie informelle dans le tiers monde.* Paris: Editions La Découverte.

Maluquer de Motes, J. (2014). *La Economia Española en Perspectiva Historica.* Barcelona: Ediciones de Pasado y Presente.

Marzin, R. (2015, Juin 10). *La biométrie électorale en Afrique (dossier).* Retrieved from https://regardexcentrique.wordpress.com/

Mbengue, M. (2009, Décembre). Enjeux et pratiques de la gouvernance électronique en Afrique de l'Ouest. *IFLA*.

Michalet, C.-A. (2004). *Qu'est-ce que la mondialisation ? : Petit traité à l'usage de ceux et celles qui ne savent pas encore s'il faut être pour ou contre.* Paris: Editions La Découverte.

Molénat, X. (2007, Décembre). Les classes moyennes. *Sciences Humaines, N°188.*

Moudio, R. (2013, May). Nigeria's film industry : a potential gold mine ? *Africa Renewal*, p. 24.

Naka, L. (1989). *Le tiers-monde et la crise d'endettement des années 80 - Fléchissement des flux financiers en direction des pays en développement : Préface de Valéry Giscard d'Estaing.* Paris, France: L'Harmattan.

National Information Technology Development Agency (NITDA). (n.d.). *2012-2014 Annual Report.*

National Institute of Statistics (Côte d'Ivoire). (2013). *A survey of the transport demand in Abidjan : household survey.*

Ndoye, M. (2006). In J.-C. Berthélemy, & A. Coulibaly, *Culture et développement en Afrique.* L'Harmattan.

NEPAD. (2014, April 27). *Plan Stratégique 2014-2017.* Retrieved from Council on Foreign Relations: www.cfr.org/china/china-africa/p9557

Nigerian Communication Commission. (n.d.). *2014 Year end subscriber/network data report for telecommunications operating companies in Nigeria : Policy Competition and Economic Analysis Department.*

Nocetti, J. (2013, Septembre - Octobre). L'irruption des réseaux sociaux sur la scène internationale. *Questions Internationales*(63).

Nwangwu, C. (2015). *Biometric voting technology and the 2015 general elections in Nigeria.* INEC.

Oxford Business Group. (2016, Juin 29). La Côte d'ivoire s'attaque au déficit des logements .

Parker, G., Van Alstyne, M., & Choudary, S. (2016). *Platform Revolution.* Norton & Co.

Pony, L. (2011). *Créer une entreprise en Afrique : Itinéraire et business plan.* Cameroun: L'Harmattan.

RAMES 2013. (2012). *Gouverner aujourd'hui ?*. Paris: DUNOD - IFRI.

RAMSES 2016. (2015). *Climat, une nouvelle chance ?*. Paris: DUNOD-IFRI.

Small, G., & Vorgan, G. (2009). *El cerebro digital: Cómo las nuevas tecnologias están cambiando nuestra mente.* Urano.

Soulé-Kohndou, F. (2013). Histoire contemporaine des relations Sud-Sud. Les contours d'une évolution graduelle. *Afrique contemporaine*(n°248), pp. 108-111.

Sparrow, P., Brewster, C., & Harris, H. (2004). *Globalizing Human Resource Management.* Routledge.

Stiglitz, J. (2010). *Freefall : America, free markets, and the sinking of the world economy.* USA: Norton & Company.

Sundararajan, A. (2016). *The sharing Economy: The end of employment and the rise of crowd-based capitalism.* Cambridge, MA, USA: MIT Press.

UNECA. (2013). *Africa-BRICS cooperation : Implications for growth, employment and structural transformation in Africa.* United Nations Economic Commission for Africa, Addis Ababa.

UN-HABITAT. (2010, March 18). *State of the world's cities 2010/2011 : Bridging the Urban Divide.* UN-HABITAT. Retrieved from UN HABITAT: mirror.unhabitat.org/documents/SOWC10/R7.pdf

UNICEF. (2014). *Rapport Régional Afrique de l'Ouest et du Centre : Tous les enfants à l'école d'ici 2015.*

Whittlesey, D. (1937, January). British and French Colonial Technique in West Africa. *Foreign Affairs.*

Wrong, M. (2002). *In the footsteps of Mr. Kurtz : living on the brink of disaster in Mobutu's Congo.* New York: Perennial edition.

Zaccheus, O. (2013, April). Understanding Oil Subsidy in Nigeria. *The spectrum: A Scolars Day Journal, 2*(Article 13).

---

www.ingramcontent.com/pod-product-compliance
Lightning Source LLC
Chambersburg PA
CBHW070308230526
45470CB00002B/773